FIREARMS
THE HISTORY OF GUNS

With an introduction by Frederick Wilkinson

Galley Press

Contents

The photographs in this book were taken by G Dagli Orti, with the exception of nos. 1, 25, 29, 30, 46, 47, 53, 54, 57–61, 63, 65–69, 71, 75, 77–80, 85, 89, 90, 92, 93, 96, 105, 106, which were supplied by the author.

Diagrams in the introduction by F Russo. Photographs in the introduction from the collection of Frederick Wilkinson.

We would like to thank the Poldi Pezzoli Museum, Milan, (photo nos. 4, 6, 9, 14–16, 41, 42, 62), the National Artillery Museum of Turin (2, 3, 5, 7, 28, 50, 55, 56, 70, 72–76, 86, 87, 91, 94, 95, 97–104), the Antiquarian 'Alle Antiche Armi' of Milan (29, 46, 54, 57, 59, 65–69, 77–80, 90, 92, 96), and private collectors in Milan and Turin for supplying the arms photographed.
From the Italian of Aldo G Cimarelli

© Istituto Geografico de Agostini, Novara 1972
English edition © Orbis Publishing Limited, London 1973
Published in this edition 1981 by
Galley Press, an imprint of W H Smith and Son Limited
Registered No. 237811 England
Trading as WHS Distributors,
St John's House, East Street,
Leicester, LE1 6NE

Printed in Italy by New Interlitho, Milan
ISBN 0-86136-001-X

Far too much of the story of man's development is taken up with accounts of his violence, both personal and national, and his attempts to destroy his fellow men. With this object in view he produced any number of ingenious and highly unpleasant devices, but for thousands of years his armoury was largely restricted to a variety of cutting and thrusting weapons. During the fourteenth century a new weapon was to make its European debût and, although it was inaccurate and unreliable, it was to change the face of war.

The development of the gun from the first inefficient models to the accurate, automatic, high velocity rifles of our time is a fascinating story. Involved are unusual characters such as Mr. Puckle, an eighteenth century firearms designer, who felt that round bullets were not really right for infidels and advocated the use of square ones against them, reserving round ones for fellow Christians. At the other extreme there was Samuel Colt whose name became synonymous with revolvers, and who introduced modern methods into the firearms industry.

Until the nineteenth century virtually every firearm was unique, for they were hand-made and represented the joint efforts of a number of craftsmen. Some of the earlier wheel-locks, especially those hunting rifles cherished by the nobility, incorporated the work of perhaps half a dozen top class engravers, inlayers, etchers, woodcarvers and jewellers. Germany rather monopolized this market at first, but later Italian craftsmen were to excel in the quality of their steelwork.

Despite their beauty, most firearms were completely functional and the gunsmiths were constantly searching for ways to improve their efficiency. Often their efforts produced some highly ingenious, if totally impractical, weapons which could well have been as great a danger to the user as the target. Others were extremely practical but were not generally adopted; as early as 1775 a British army officer, Captain Patrick Ferguson, produced and, most convincingly, demonstrated a breech-loading flint-lock rifle. He met his death in the American revolutionary war, and his ingenious rifle was forgotten (the industry tended to be rather conservative).

By the end of the eighteenth century almost every idea had been explored, even if not exploited. It was a Scottish cleric who made the next great innovation, that changed the entire industry and pointed the way to the modern cartridge weapon.

During the long history of firearms a few weapons acquired a reputation which has survived them by centuries. There was the standard British army musket, Brown Bess, which saw service on battlefields in India, China, and America as well as Europe. The blunderbuss can be recognized by everybody but there are many myths about that weapon; while the imagination of many people is stirred by the sight of a pair of duelling pistols.

All these and many other fascinating weapons are described in the text whilst more than one hundred, high quality colour plates illustrate some of the best examples of European and American firearms.

English brass-barrelled blunderbuss, c. 1700.

The origin of gunpowder

One of the first lessons that man learned was that the greater the distance at which you could strike your foe, the better were your chances of victory. If the enemy was near enough for hand-to-hand fighting he was far too close! No doubt the first missile was a stone, but during the Mesolithic period prehistoric man discovered the possibilities of using a springy piece of wood, and so the bow was born. This weapon greatly increased the length of a man's reach, and until the fourteenth century it was to remain the main missile arm.

The Romans developed the bow, and used large crossbows which were powerful enough to discharge a spear or a large rock. Warriors in ancient and medieval times extended the idea of missile arms with catapults, which could hurl great stones against the fortified walls of a town or castle; but these weapons entailed severe limitations, for they were heavy, cumbersome and had to be constructed on the site, requiring the services of a large number of craftsmen. Even the longbow had its disadvantages, for it required hours of practice and great skill for its effective management. The crossbow required less skill, but it was slow in use and far more complex in construction.

The answer to all these handicaps and drawbacks was to appear first in China. The origin of gunpowder is still obscure although, thanks to the modern research, it seems fairly certain that this highly combustible mixture of charcoal, potassium nitrate and sulphur was first compounded in China. The earliest recorded use of it seems to have been in the eleventh century. The potential of this new weapon was not at first appreciated by the Chinese, who used it primarily as a psychological weapon; the flash, the smoke and the bang being intended merely to frighten the enemy. However, the Chinese warrior soon saw that the explosion could be used to propel small objects, and by about the middle of the twelfth century they had developed some simple form of gun. It was probably a strengthened piece of hollow bamboo into

which were forced powder and balls of clay, small stones or cast bullets. The effect of a number of these weapons being discharged at an unprepared enemy was, no doubt, quite remarkable for in addition to fire, smoke and smell, death struck unseen. It is not therefore surprising that knowledge of this new weapon began to spread amongst the war-like nations of the East, and it is probably thanks to the Arabs that knowledge of this new powder reached Europe.

It can be said with certainty that early in the fourteenth century, cannon were in use in Europe, for there are two references of 1326; one documentary, and the other a picture of a crude cannon. Once the idea of a cannon ejecting a missile had been grasped by the medieval militarists, development was fairly rapid. The illustration of 1326 shows a vase-shaped cannon, but soon more conventional, cylindrical barrels were being used. Larger and larger cannon were made but smaller versions, hand guns, were also produced. These were simply small barrels with a hole, the touch-hole, drilled through the side. A charge of powder was poured down from the muzzle and pushed home into the breech, followed by a bullet of lead, iron or even a small arrow, rammed down to sit firmly on top of the powder. A small amount of powder, the priming, was now placed over the touch-hole and this was then ignited by a piece of smouldering moss, a burning cord or a hot iron. As the priming flared the flame passed through the touch-hole to the main charge of powder inside the barrel which exploded and so drove out the bullet. The hand gun was fitted to a wooden or metal body, the stock, so that it could be handled with reasonable safety.

These early hand guns were crude but tremendously important, for the only skill required to operate them was the ability to measure off an amount of powder and to point the weapon in the right direction. Certainly they were inaccurate, but armed with them, a number of completely untrained peasants could be turned into a formidable striking force in a very short time. Furthermore the penetrating power of the bullet was

5

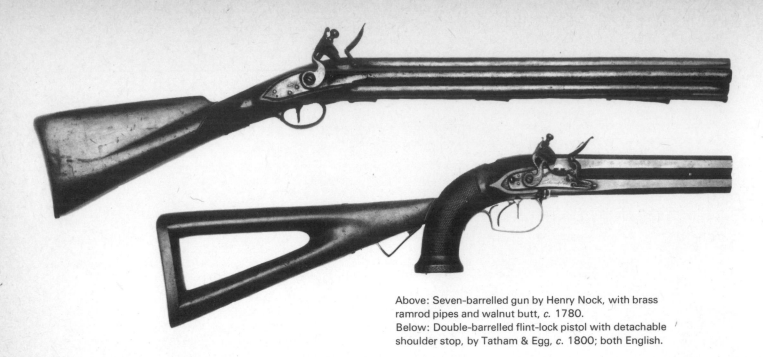

Above: Seven-barrelled gun by Henry Nock, with brass ramrod pipes and walnut butt, *c.* 1780.
Below: Double-barrelled flint-lock pistol with detachable shoulder stop, by Tatham & Egg, *c.* 1800; both English.

considerable and at close range it was strong enough to penetrate all but the thickest and best-made armour. The introduction of gunpowder gradually rendered armour obsolete, until by the seventeenth century it had been abandoned almost everywhere.

Hand guns were limited in use since the gunner needed a supply of powder and, far more important, a means of ignition. There was considerable difficulty in keeping the burning moss or cord alight, in addition to the sheer physical problem of being able to place it directly onto the touch-hole. The first step in overcoming these limitations was the introduction of the match, probably late in the fourteenth century. It consisted of a piece of cord soaked in a solution of saltpetre and then dried, so that if the tip were lit, the cord smouldered slowly and stayed alight for a considerable length of time. The next step was the introduction of a mechanical means of applying the match directly to the touch-hole and priming: this was the serpentine, an S-shaped arm fixed to the side of the stock. The glowing end of the match was placed in the top arm of the S, and, as the arm was pivoted at the centre, pressure on the lower end caused the top to swing forward – pressing the glowing tip of the match into the priming powder. Another very effective modification was the introduction of the priming pan. Instead of the touch-hole being on top of the barrel as previously, it was now positioned at the side, just above a small metal pan fitted to the side of the barrel. Into the pan was placed the priming, and a small metal plate could be swung to cover the pan and so preserve the priming from wind or rain.

The musket

By the middle of the sixteenth century the match-lock musket was fitted with a barrel about four feet long, and fired a bullet about three quarters of an inch in diameter. The long barrel was fitted to a sturdy wooden stock, the end of which was shaped so that the piece could now be held to the shoulder and an effective aim taken. In place of the old-fashioned serpentine there was a simple arrangement of levers operated by a trigger situated below the stock which, when pressed, caused the arm holding the match to swing forward and ignite the priming. The long barrel and the wooden stock made the musket so heavy that it was difficult for a musketeer to support the weapon unaided. To overcome this, the musketeer of the late sixteenth and early seventeenth centuries carried a light wooden pole fitted with a shaped metal arm at the top, the rest, with which he could support the musket in the aiming position. The musketeer was cluttered with spare lengths of match (often carried inside the hat or tucked into the belt), a small container which held the priming powder, and possibly a second, larger powder flask, which held the main supply; as well as a small leather bag which contained a supply of bullets. If he used a powder flask each load had to be measured, and to overcome this, many used a bandolier – a series of small wooden or horn bottles suspended from a cross belt. Each of the containers held the correct amount of powder for one shot, and so did away with the need to make any measurement.

The wheel-lock

The match-lock musket changed the face of war, for no longer was the knight supreme on the battlefield; neither were the massed bodies of spearmen and axemen invincible. In their place now stood groups of men with these devastatingly noisy, yet powerful, muskets. However there were problems, for it was not easy to manage a six feet long musket, a glowing length of match, a rest and quantities of dangerously explosive gunpowder. The musketeer was also very much at the mercy of wind and weather; a sudden downpour of rain, and every match in the regiment might be extinguished. Strong gusts of wind could blow out the match; or, worse still, drift a spark into an uncovered barrel of gunpowder. What the soldier needed was a means of ignition which was not itself burning. Very early in the sixteenth century there are accounts of attempts to overcome the problem. Leonardo

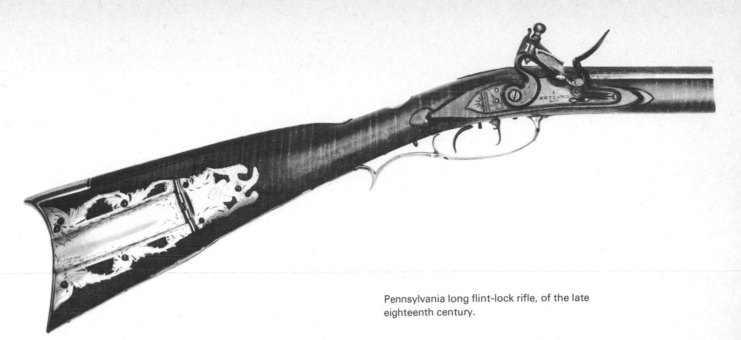

Pennsylvania long flint-lock rifle, of the late
eighteenth century.

da Vinci visualized a mechanical means of ignition by
which a piece of mineral could be scraped across a rough
metal surface, to produce tiny sparks which would fall into
the priming and so ignite the main charge.

The mechanism which was developed was known as the
wheel-lock and consisted of a solid steel wheel, perhaps
a quarter of an inch thick, the rim of which was grooved
and slotted and formed the base of the pan. The wheel
was connected by means of a short, linked chain, to a
powerful V-spring. From the centre of the wheel projected
a square lug, and over this was placed a key so that the
wheel could be turned. As the wheel was rotated it
compressed the main spring until a small metal arm, the
sear, slipped forward to lock it in position. A piece of
mineral, pyrites, was firmly held at the end of a pivoted
metal arm. To fire a shot, the main charge and bullet were
loaded; the wheel rotated; and a pinch of powder placed
in the pan. The arm was swung forward so that the pyrites
then pressed in to the priming and onto the rim of the
wheel. When the trigger was pressed the small sear was
withdrawn and the spring made the wheel rotate rapidly,
when friction between the roughened edge of the wheel
and the pyrites produced sparks.

This lock could be produced in any size. Thus was born
the pistol, the name of which is usually taken as being
derived from Pistoia, a town in Italy. One of the great
advantages of the wheel-lock was that it could be loaded
and the mechanism wound, and the weapon could then be
put to one side but was instantly ready for firing. If safety
was of prime importance then the arm holding the pyrites
could be swung clear of the pan and there was no danger
of an accidental misfire, for no sparks could be struck.
However, the expense of production was such that wheel-
lock pistols were issued only to selected cavalry units,
whilst wheel-lock guns and rifles were primarily weapons
of the rich. German and Italian smiths supplied most of
the wheel-locks which remained in use all through the
sixteenth century. Although alternative methods of
ignition were evolved, wheel-lock sporting rifles were
popular with rich sportsmen well into the seventeenth

century. This demand for an obsolete weapon was
probably maintained because of the opportunities they
afforded the gunsmith in the way of decoration. Stocks
were inlaid with horn, ivory, mother-of-pearl, and various
woods, and many of these weapons are works of art in
their own right.

The snaphaunce

The wheel-lock released the soldier and hunter from the
tyranny of fire; they were now able to travel safely and
easily, with a loaded weapon ready to hand for instant use.
It was not perfect, for the mechanism was very complex
compared with the simple match-lock and it was subject
to jamming – often, no doubt, at the most inconvenient
moment. Breakages were not the sort that could be easily
repaired in the field and production expenses were
considerable. However, once the principle of spark
ignition had been conceived, gunsmiths everywhere
experimented. Probably about 1540–1550 somebody came
up with an answer, the principle of which was the same as
for the wheel-lock; but in place of a wheel and chain and
pyrites, a simple piece of common flint and a steel plate
were all that were needed. Situated just above the pan was
a small, vertical steel plate and this was secured to the end
of a pivoted, slightly curved arm which was fitted to the
outside of the lock plate. In place of the metal arm holding
the piece of pyrites, there was the cock which held in its
jaws a small, wedge-shaped piece of flint. The operating
mechanism still consisted of a V-shaped spring, but in this
system it pressed directly on the cock rather than by
means of a connecting chain. To fire the pistol it was
necessary to place powder and bullet down the barrel and
deposit a pinch of priming into the pan, when a sliding
cover, as with the match-lock, was pushed forward to
protect the priming. The metal arm holding the plate was
positioned so that the steel plate was situated just above
the pan, and here the arm was held in place by a spring.
The cock was pulled back and locked into this rear
position by means of a small sear, much as on the wheel-

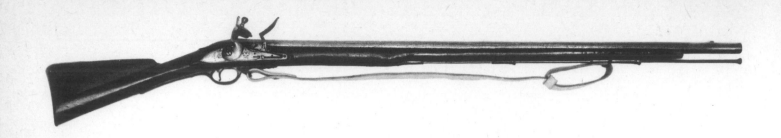

British army 'Brown Bess' flint-lock musket of India pattern, *c*. 1800.

lock, and the spring was now under tension. To fire a shot the pan cover was pushed clear and the trigger pressed; this released the cock, so that it moved forward to scrape the sharpened end of the flint down the steel plate and produce the sparks. The pressure of the cock and flint also pushed the plate clear of the pan, so allowing the sparks to fall into the priming. Soon the gunsmith had done away with this lock's one major drawback, the necessity of remembering to open the pan cover. By means of a simple internal arrangement of levers, the pan cover was automatically pushed clear. Although the name given to this action was the snaphaunce, usually derived from the Dutch 'snaaphaans', the invention appears to have been Italian.

The flint-lock

The snaphaunce represented a simplification of ignition but even this was not without its limitations, for the internal coupling and separate pan cover and steel presented certain mechanical problems. About the middle of the sixteenth century some gunmakers were experimenting with another idea, whereby the steel and the pan cover were incorporated into a single L-shaped piece of metal, usually known as the frizzen, pivoted at the end of the short arm which served as the pan cover. This had the virtue that as the flint struck against the steel, it struck sparks and also automatically pushed clear the pan cover. The adoption of this L-shaped frizzen not only reduced the chances of a misfire but also reduced the amount of internal mechanism required. However, it fell to a French gunsmith to produce the most simple, efficient, reliable and enduring lock mechanism. Marin Le Bourgeoys, a Normandy gunmaker, about the year 1610, took two simple features and combined them to produce the French lock, which was to remain standard for most firearms for the next two centuries. Le Bourgeoys' lock used the conventional L-shaped frizzen fitted above the pan on the lock plate together with the frizzen spring. On the inside of the plate was a shaped metal block, known

as the tumbler, which had a lug which passed through a hole in the plate; onto this lug was secured the cock. The large V-shaped spring bore down directly on the front of the tumbler so that a backward movement of the cock compressed the V-spring. On the rear face of the tumbler were cut two slits of slightly varying depths and angles. A small arm, the sear, which was engaged by the trigger, pressed against the face of the tumbler. As the cock was rotated the V-spring was compressed, and the end of the sear slipped into the first notch. This was so designed that pressure on the trigger would not disengage the sear, which meant that the action could not be operated. This safety position was known as the half-cock. If the cock were now pulled a little further to the rear, the sear automatically disengaged from the first slit and slipped into the second. This one was so shaped that pressure on the trigger would withdraw the sear and allow the main spring to rotate the tumbler and hence the cock, which swung forward to strike sparks from the flint and frizzen.

The French lock was the basic means of ignition on which firearms designers were to depend right up to the early nineteenth century, although there were variations on the theme. The Spanish produced what was known as a 'miquelet' lock and this differed in that the mainspring was situated on the outside of the lock plate and bore directly on the toe of the cock. There were also differences in the method of engaging half- and full cock; the half-cock position was held by a small arm or sear which projected through the lock plate to engage with the cock. The other differences were in details of shape, for on the French lock the flint was usually held by two semi-oval jaws whereas the Spanish favoured square-cut jaws. The mainspring on these 'miquelet' locks was rather strong and, in order to offer a firm grip for the finger and thumb, the cock was fitted with a ring or a small shaped metal bar which afforded an extra purchase.

During the seventeenth century there was a peculiarly English variation on the French lock, which consisted of a little hook fitted behind the cock on the lock plate. This hook engaged with a notch on the rear of the cock in the

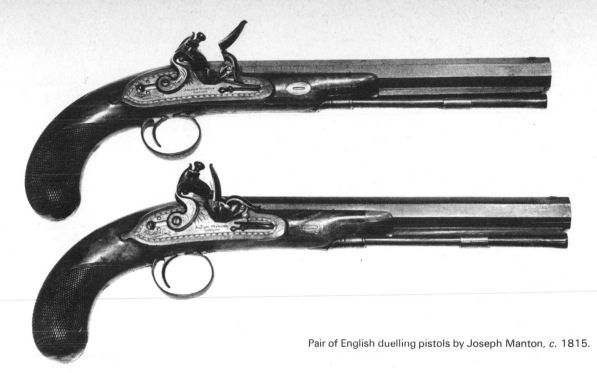

Pair of English duelling pistols by Joseph Manton, *c.* 1815.

half-cock position, so giving a double safety device. This little catch was known as the dog.

During the seventeenth century, although the mechanism remained the same, there were changes in the shape of the flint-lock. Those dating from around the middle of the century had flat lock plates and flat-sided cocks, and there was a distinct down-drooping shape to the lock plate. Towards the end of the century the banana shape became a little more pronounced, whereas both the cock and the lock plate took on a half-rounded section.

Military and civilian guns

The eighteenth century may be said to be the age of the flint-lock, for during this period almost every possible facet of its development was explored by the various gunmakers. In northern Italy, around Brescia, the craftsmen continued to produce superb quality snaphaunce pistols, but elsewhere in Europe the flint-lock reigned supreme. Flint-lock muskets became standard issue for almost all the infantry, whilst the cavalry were armed with a pair of pistols carried in saddle holsters. It was a time of lawlessness and no traveller moved far without at least one pistol secreted in his pocket or hung at his belt. Shooting also became a sport, and for the landed gentry with money to spare there were superbly made, single or double barrelled fowling pieces. These fine weapons were available from the master gunmakers of London and Birmingham, but for the greater part of the eighteenth century it was London that dominated the British firearms industry. During the early part of the century most of the London gunsmiths were to be found situated in that part of the town near the Tower of London, because the greatest demand for firearms naturally came from the army. As London developed, some of the craftsmen moved further west and set up shops in Piccadilly and Oxford Street and the newly built-up areas of London.

Of course weapons intended for the civilian market were far more decorative and elaborate than those intended for military use; these were, by necessity, plainer and far more rugged in order to stand up to the far harder usage they received. At the end of the first quarter of the eighteenth century the musket was adopted which remained, in various patterns, the standard issue of the British Army for the next hundred years: the Brown Bess. During its long life it underwent a number of minor changes of detail, but the basic weapon remained unchanged. The earliest models were fitted with 46 inch barrels, but it was found that as the quality of gunpowder was improved this great length of barrel was unnecessary and shorter, 42 inch barrels were introduced. Later, under the severe pressure and enormous demand of the Napoleonic wars, cheaper, simpler and shorter-barrelled versions were produced. For the greater part of the Napoleonic wars the British infantry carried the 39 inch Brown Bess which was often inaccurate, but usually thoroughly mechanically reliable. The musket could be converted into a short pike by the fitting of a triangular-bladed bayonet, which was slipped over the muzzle. There was also a reduction in the size of barrels fitted to the cavalry pistols; the earlier versions mostly had 12 inch barrels, later reduced to nine inch. Naval pistols, usually referred to as sea service weapons, were frequently fitted with a long bar on the side of the stock and this belt hook enabled the user to carry the pistol at his belt without using a holster.

The so-called Queen Anne pistol, which enjoyed great popularity with civilians, differed from the military version in a number of ways. The general standard of workmanship was superior and they were normally far more decorative. Despite their name the manufacture of these pistols continued long after the death of Queen Anne in 1714. Most had a barrel which screwed on to a metal breech, on the side of which was fitted the frizzen and spring. Only the butt was of wood, and this was usually embellished with a silver butt cap, commonly a grotesque head, and decorated with silver wire which was let into the wood. A small channel was cut into the wood and the silver wire was pressed home, and then gently hammered

Percussion system pocket pistol, by William Parker
of London, *c.* 1820.

so that it swelled to grip the sides of the channel. Since
the barrels could be unscrewed, allowing direct access to
the breech, powder and ball could be loaded without
recourse to the use of a ramrod.

Blunderbuss and rifle

Very popular for house protection, and with guards on
stage coaches, was the blunderbuss. The blunderbuss was
introduced during the sixteenth century and continued in
use well up to the early part of the nineteenth century. Its
main feature was a barrel, the bore of which widened
towards the muzzle; this effect was achieved either by
having a cylindrical barrel and increasing the diameter of
the bore as it approached the muzzle, or by fitting a
barrel in which the wall was of uniform thickness but was
belled at the muzzle. One virtue claimed for the
blunderbuss was ease of loading, as the wide muzzle
facilitated the insertion of powder and shot, the normal
charge being around 15 to 20 small lead balls. Secondly, it
was thought that the wide muzzle would spread the shot as
it left the barrel; in fact the spread of shot due to the
widening of the bore was minimal. Many blunderbusses
were fitted with bayonets which could be folded back
along the barrel. A small catch secured the blade, and
when released the bayonet was swung forward by a
spring and locked into position ready for action.

One of the greatest limitations of flint-lock firearms was
that they were almost invariably single shot, and when
this had been fired there was a considerable delay while
the gun was reloaded and reprimed ready for a second
shot. Many attempts were made by gunmakers to
overcome this problem. Simplest and probably most
effective was the use of two or more barrels on the
weapon, usually with one barrel fitted above the other.
During the seventeenth century and early part of the
eighteenth century, the barrels were rotated so that each
was brought, in turn, to line up with the cock ready for
firing. During the latter part of the eighteenth century
another system, using the so-called 'tap action', was

adopted. Here two barrels, one above the other, were
connected to the touch-hole by means of a small channel
drilled through a circular block, the tap, set into the
breech. With the tap in one position the lower barrel was
sealed off from the pan, and if the action were cocked and
fired the sparks fell into the priming pan and discharged
the top barrel. By rotating the tap through 90 degrees by
means of a small side arm, a second charge of priming was
brought into position and this was connected, via the small
drilled hole, to the lower barrel; the action was then
re-cocked and fired and the second barrel discharged. The
same principle was occasionally incorporated in a few
three-barrelled pistols.

Other more ingenious and often less practical ideas
were used to produce multishot weapons, among them the
superimposed charge. In weapons of this type a charge of
powder and ball was rammed home into the breech,
followed by a wad, and then a second charge of powder
and ball were rammed home. The barrel was drilled with
two touch-holes and frequently fitted with two locks,
although on some models the one lock was made
movable so that it could be used to discharge both shots.
When the lock was cocked it fired the priming, which was
connected to the front charge and bullet. This was fired,
and it was hoped and believed that the wad was sufficient
protection to keep the flash from the second charge. The
lock was then moved back, primed and cocked and on
firing this time the second shot was discharged. Some of
these superimposed loads incorporated two, three, four or
more charges.

Flint-lock pistols were also incorporated into other
weapons, the most popular of which was the sword pistol.
Usually a short-bladed sword was fitted at the hilt with
the barrel, trigger and cock of a small flint-lock pistol;
thus the weapon could be used as a sword, but in an
emergency the blade could be pointed at the target and
the pistol discharged.

It cannot be claimed with any degree of authority that
the majority of flint-lock weapons were accurate. Most
were smooth-bored which meant that the bullet 'rolled'

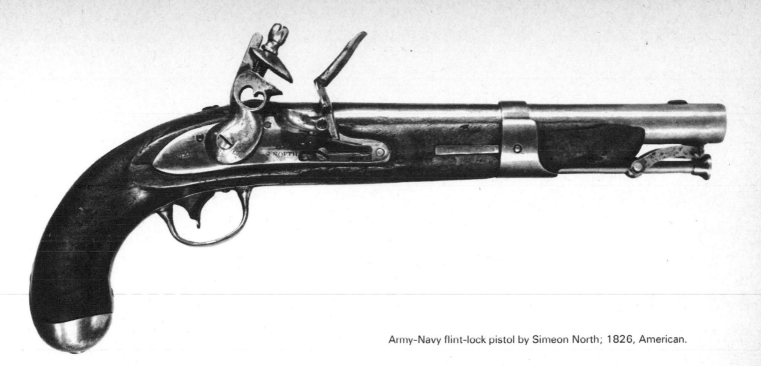

Army-Navy flint-lock pistol by Simeon North; 1826, American.

along and might wobble in flight, with consequent loss of accuracy. From the sixteenth century it was realized that if a bullet could be made to rotate in flight, this spin helped to even out variations in the line of flight. The problem was how to achieve this rotation. The simplest method was by the use of rifling, when a series of shallow grooves were cut on the inside face of the barrel. The bullet was made to fit very tightly, being forced home, and as it was of soft lead it expanded to fill the rifling grooves. When the shot was discharged the bullet was forced out of the barrel, and since the grooves were cut in a spiral fashion the bullet followed this path and was indeed spinning as it left the muzzle. The technical problems involved in cutting the rifling were so difficult that rifles were comparatively uncommon. During the latter part of the eighteenth century there was to emerge the American rifle par excellence: known, rather erroneously, as the Kentucky rifle and, more correctly, as the Pennsylvanian long rifle. This weapon was a combination of American ingenuity and European skill and craftsmanship. During the formative years of the American colonies, many Europeans emigrated and settled there and among them were German and Austrian gunsmiths with experience in making rifles. In their new country they gradually evolved a peculiarly American style of weapon which had a very long, heavy, rifled barrel which fired a small calibre ball. They were powerful and very accurate, and during the American War of Independence (1775–1783) these Pennsylvanian long rifles proved a considerable hazard to the British troops.

Another specialized form of firearm which evolved towards the end of the eighteenth century was the duelling pistol, designed to be reliable and accurate. Locks were fitted with every refinement to ensure swift action, while the barrels were heavy and carefully drilled (although English duellists rather frowned on the use of rifling). The stock was mostly plain, with perhaps just a little hatching on the butt to help maintain a good grip. Often the trigger guard was fitted with a spur intended to provide a purchase for the second finger. In order to ensure equal chances for both participants, duelling pistols were sold in matched pairs in a wooden box fitted with all necessary accessories.

The percussion principle

Although the flint-lock proved itself to be extremely adaptable it was not without its drawbacks. First and foremost was the necessity to have a good, sharp flint, for normally each piece was reckoned to be reliable for a maximum of thirty shots. There was the constant danger of the frizzen jamming or the flint failing to strike sparks from the face of the steel. For the sportsman, perhaps even more important was the so-called hang-fire; when the trigger was pressed the flint struck sparks from the face of the steel; these fell into and ignited the priming, which flared up and the flame travelled very quickly through the touch-hole to set off the main charge. These actions took only a fraction of a second but the sum total was an appreciable delay. This meant that the sportsman taking aim at a moving target pressed the trigger and, because of this hang-fire, the shot was appreciably delayed so that by the time the bullet left the barrel the marksman might well be off aim.

There was, in Scotland, a parish clergyman by the name of Alexander Forsyth who was concerned with this problem of the hang-fire and, being something of an amateur chemist, he experimented with the use of explosive fulminates. These chemicals are unstable and require only a blow to produce a minor explosion. The reverend Forsythe produced an ingenious, if somewhat complicated, system of using these fulminates as a means to ignite a main charge. Fitted over the touch-hole was a hollow metal block known, from its shape, as the scent bottle, containing a small quantity of fulminate of mercury. When this was fitted at the side of the barrel and inverted, small grains of fulminate ran out through the nozzle and were placed over the touch-hole. When the trigger was pressed a solid-nosed hammer swung forward, and struck, via a spring-loaded plunger, the fulminate

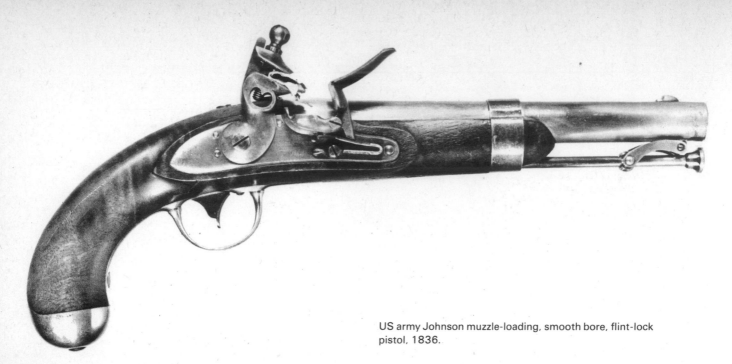

US army Johnson muzzle-loading, smooth bore, flint-lock pistol, 1836.

which exploded and produced a tiny flame sufficient to ignite the main charge. The scent bottle worked: the hang-fire period was reduced, but there were still snags in the design. The scent bottle mechanism was delicate and there was always the danger that the entire amount of fulminate could be exploded and cause a minor accident. Some time during the first quarter of the nineteenth century a gunsmith came up with the idea of depositing a tiny quantity of fulminate on the inside of a small copper cap. This metal cap was held in place by friction on the nipple, which was a pillar of metal drilled with a hole and screwed into place over the touch-hole. In place of the old cock a solid-nosed metal hammer was used, but the internal mechanism was identical with that of a flint-lock. Once the firearm had been loaded with a charge of powder and shot, one of these small metal caps was placed over the nipple. The hammer was now pulled back to the full cock position and the trigger pressed, allowing it to swing forward, strike the metal cap and explode the deposit of fulminate inside. The flash passed down the communicating hole and so fired the main charge. By 1820 the percussion lock had largely captured the firearms market for it was simple, convenient and greatly reduced the number of misfires. There were some drawbacks: the cap was rather small, and therefore difficult to handle with gloved hands.

The small copper percussion cap opened the way for a whole flood of innovations in firearms design; possibly the most important was the ability to produce practical, reliable revolvers. These had been made in the past – indeed, some of the earliest firearms had incorporated the 'revolver' principle, but the difficulties raised by the necessity of having frizzens, springs and cocks, had proved too difficult; no really satisfactory model was devised until the 1830s–1840s. The simplest form of revolver was the so-called pepperbox. Here a solid metal cylinder, some four or five inches long, was drilled with a number of chambers which did not pass right through the block, but were connected to a nipple by means of a small touch-hole at the rear. Each chamber was loaded

with powder and ball and a cap placed on the nipple; then, either mechanically or manually, the cylinder was rotated and pressure on the trigger allowed a hammer to fall and strike a nipple, and so fire the charge. Releasing the trigger and pulling it back again rotated the cylinder until the next nipple was in line with the hammer, and the process could be repeated until all five or six chambers had been emptied. Some so-called transition revolvers, produced around the middle of the nineteenth century, took the same basic idea but had a short cylinder with a barrel fitted just in front.

The first Colt revolvers

The first practical and efficient percussion revolver was that produced by 'Colonel' Samuel Colt. A hard-headed Yankee from Hartford, Connecticut, he was a natural entrepreneur and was prepared to dabble in anything which stimulated his interest and offered a profit. It was during a long sea voyage that he conceived and modelled a revolver mechanism. The first of his models, the Paterson Colt, was produced in 1836 but, despite its obvious advantages, it did not find an immediate market. However, by good luck, good public relations and hard work, Colt's revolvers finally made the grade and from 1847 onwards a steady supply of good quality percussion revolvers came from Colt's factory. Most were six-shots with single action mechanism, i.e. the hammer had to be pulled back by the thumb, and this movement rotated the cylinder and cocked the action. Pressure on the trigger allowed the hammer to fall forward, strike the nipple and so discharge the shot. Colt's factory later produced double action revolvers, which meant that the weapon could be operated in exactly the same way as the earlier single action, or by an alternative method which carried out the same action automatically with pressure on the trigger. In England, Colt's rivals were men such as Tranter, Webley, Adams and others, all of whom produced fine quality percussion revolvers. The great majority of these revolvers were sold, like the duelling pistols, in cases. The

Percussion revolver by Adams of London, *c.* 1850.

adoption of the percussion revolver ousted the blunderbuss from its prime position as a house defence weapon, and very few were produced from the 1820s onwards.

Another problem which had long defeated the firearms designers was the ability to load from the breech. Most of the early breech-loading weapons used the idea of a detachable chamber, which was usually in the form of a mug with a handle. Each was loaded with powder and ball and then placed at the rear of the barrel, secured in place and the shot fired. The empty chamber was removed and a fresh one put back in position. This system was reasonable for cannon and larger weapons where the chamber could be jammed very securely against the base of the barrel, but for pistols and long arms the gas leakage around the joint was quite considerable; apart from being a potential danger to the user, it also meant that there was a loss of power. From the sixteenth to eighteenth centuries there had been many experiments but all had, for various reasons, proved unacceptable. One of the most efficient systems was the Ferguson breech-loading rifle, designed in 1774 by Captain Patrick Ferguson. The basic principle was a plug which could be unscrewed, allowing direct access to the breech into which powder and ball were placed, and then by rotating the trigger guard the plug was replaced and the weapon was ready for firing. This was a very efficient weapon but was not generally adopted. When the percussion cap was introduced the military planners were, quite understandably, a little reluctant to rush in to mass production before the system had proved itself, and it was not until 1839 that the British army officially adopted the percussion principle. Most of the military firearms of this time were still smooth bore, but the Crimean War demonstrated to the main military powers of Europe the great deficiencies of smooth bore weapons. The Enfield Small Arms Factory, just outside London, was charged with the responsibility of producing efficient rifles. As a result of their experiments the Enfield percussion rifle was produced in 1853. Firing a large diameter (.577) bullet it was an efficient weapon, but still suffered from the great handicap of being muzzle-loading.

Experimenters in all European countries had been busily engaged in the search for a solution, in 1841 the Dreyse rifle was produced. Its impact was considerable. This weapon used a bolt which was a metal block at the breech which could be opened to allow a paper cartridge, containing powder, a percussion cap embedded within the powder, and a bullet, to be placed directly in the breech. The bolt was then closed and when the trigger was pressed a long, thin needle pierced the paper of the cartridge and struck the percussion cap, which ignited and detonated the charge. Prussia used this weapon with devastating effect in her wars, and the impact on warfare in general was quite remarkable. Other attempts to introduce cartridges were made by the Frenchman Lefaucheux in 1835, using a small amount of fulminate deposited on the inside of a small metal cartridge. It was struck by a small metal pin, but this meant that it only fitted weapons adapted to take this particular cartridge.

It was with the introduction of the metal-cased cartridge in 1854 that a real solution came to the hands of the firearms designer. By the 1860s the modern metal-cased cartridge, with the percussion cap fitted centrally in the base, was available. As the cartridge designer and producer gained more experience, so stronger and better-fitting cartridges were produced. Military planners in all countries searched desperately for a really efficient breech-loading rifle. In Britain, after many experiments, the Martini Henry Rifle was produced. As a result of various tests the Martini action, which made use of a block which was lowered by depressing the trigger guard, so allowing direct access to the breech, was fitted with a Henry barrel and was officially adopted by the British Army in 1871. This weapon saw service in most of Britain's colonies and in frontier wars.

The Martini Henry came in for a good deal of criticism, some unjustified, but the path was now mapped and by the end of the nineteenth century the short magazine Lee Enfield rifle had been adopted. Here was a rifle firing quite a small diameter bullet, .303, with

Winchester: calibre .45 (70) carbine, 1886 model.

accuracy and with a good, efficient bolt system which reduced leakage to an absolute minimum. Furthermore the efficiency and usefulness of the weapon had been greatly increased, because it was no longer a single shot weapon; a metal container fitted beneath the breech held ten cartridges. This was not a new idea, for as early as 1860 the Henry rifle had demonstrated quite clearly that magazine rifles were within the capabilities of the firearms industry. The most famous of all repeating rifles was the Winchester, which was first produced in 1866. In this particular model the cartridges were held in a cylindrical magazine situated beneath the barrel. A new cartridge was fed into the breech, and the empty case removed and ejected by operating a lever situated beneath the butt.

When a cartridge is detonated the bullet is ejected and there is an equal reaction in the opposite direction. This kick, or recoil, had long been regarded as nothing more than a nuisance, but Hugo Borchardt conceived the idea of using the recoil to operate a mechanism which would extract the spent cartridge and replace it with a fresh one. In 1893 the Borchardt self-loading pistol was produced in Berlin; it used a rather involved and complicated

mechanism which was not really practical, but clearly indicated the line of future development. This method was modified by George Luger, who in 1898 produced the pistol which bore his name and was to continue in production right up to 1942. The action was rather complex, depending on a toggle arm which might well be damaged. In 1897 another great firearms designer, John Browning, produced a self-loading pistol, but it was not generally adopted, and in 1900 the famous Colt factory entered the field. After a number of experiments and changes in design the famous .45 Colt automatic pistol was produced in 1911, probably one of the best known firearms in the world. On this weapon the recoil is used to drive a metal slide back, which is returned by a spring; this backward and forward movement extracts the empty case, ejects it and reloads a new cartridge from the magazine housed in the butt.

The development and use of hand guns and other firearms in the twentieth century, and their effect on modern warfare, is another story, and perhaps an all too familiar one. The old Chinese genius who first stuffed a bamboo tube with his 'magic' mixture could hardly have dreamed of the outcome of his invention.

Bibliography

Blair, C. *European and American Arms*, Batsford 1962; *Pistols of the World*, Batsford 1968
Blackmore, H. *Guns and Rifles of the World*, Batsford 1965; *Hunting Weapons*, Barrie & Jenkins 1971
Bailey, D. W. *Percussion Guns and Rifles*, Arms & Armour Press, 1972

Hayward, J. F. *The Art of the Gunmaker, Vols 1 & 2*, Barrie & Rockliff 1963 & 1965
Peterson, H. *Encyclopedia of Firearms*, New York 1964
Taylerson, A. *Revolving Arms*, Herbert Jenkins 1967
Wilkinson, F. *Small Arms*, Ward Lock 1966; *Flintlock Pistols*, Arms & Armour Press 1968; *Flintlock Guns and Rifles*, Arms & Armour Press 1971; *Guns*, Hamlyn 1970

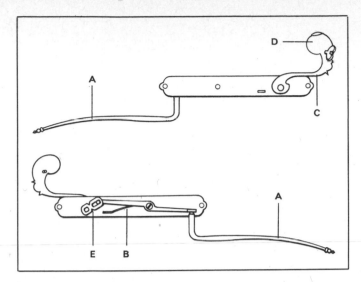

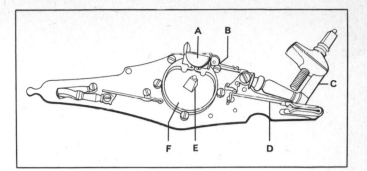

Wheel-lock mechanism. A: pan; B: pan cover (open); C: cock (in the safe position, but without the pyrites in its jaws); D: spring to hold cock in fire position; E: lug of the wheel onto which the winding spanner fits; F: wheel cover.

Match-lock. A: trigger; B: sear spring; C: serpentine; D: match clamp; E: cam. Pressure on the trigger rotates the cam and allows the serpentine to swing forward and down into the firing pan.

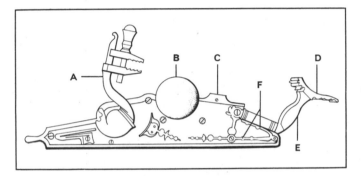

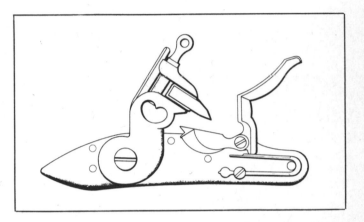

Flint-lock mechanism of French military rifle, 1777 model. This type of robust mechanism was in use until the invention of the percussion system.

Dutch snaphaunce. A: cock; B: pan, with its characteristic end cover; C: pan cover (open); D: steel; E: steel arm (in safe position); F: steel spring.

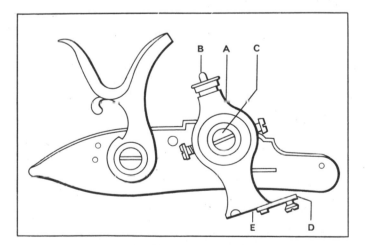

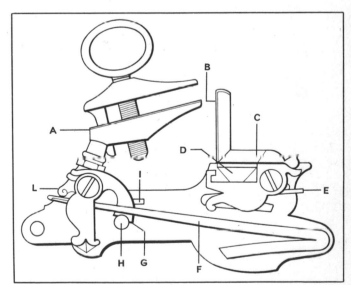

Forsyth scent-bottle. A: scent-bottle; B: striker; C: pivot on which the scent-bottle revolves; D: revolving cover of the fulminate magazine at the bottom of the scent-bottle; E: loading hole for fulminate.

Spanish 'miquelet'. A: cock; B: frizzen; C: pan cover; D: pan; E: frizzen spring; F: main-spring; G: toe; H: sear, on which the cock rests in the safety position; I: primary sear on which the toe rests when it is cocked, ready for firing; L: heel, which is driven forward by the main-spring when the trigger is pulled.

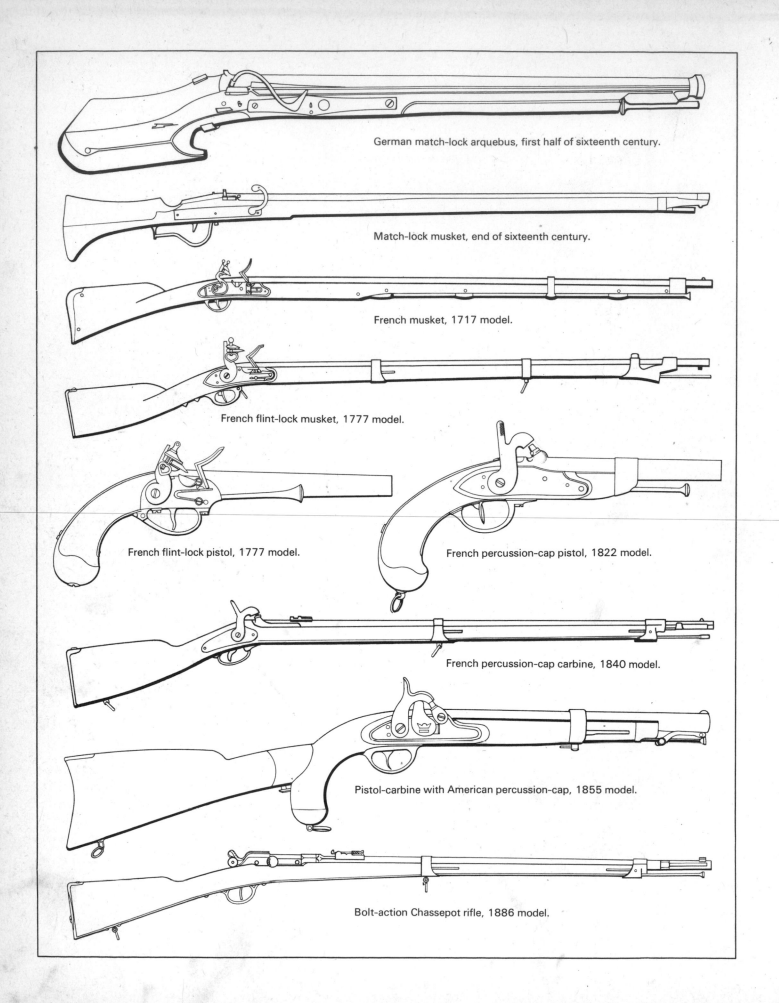

German match-lock arquebus, first half of sixteenth century.

Match-lock musket, end of sixteenth century.

French musket, 1717 model.

French flint-lock musket, 1777 model.

French flint-lock pistol, 1777 model.

French percussion-cap pistol, 1822 model.

French percussion-cap carbine, 1840 model.

Pistol-carbine with American percussion-cap, 1855 model.

Bolt-action Chassepot rifle, 1886 model.

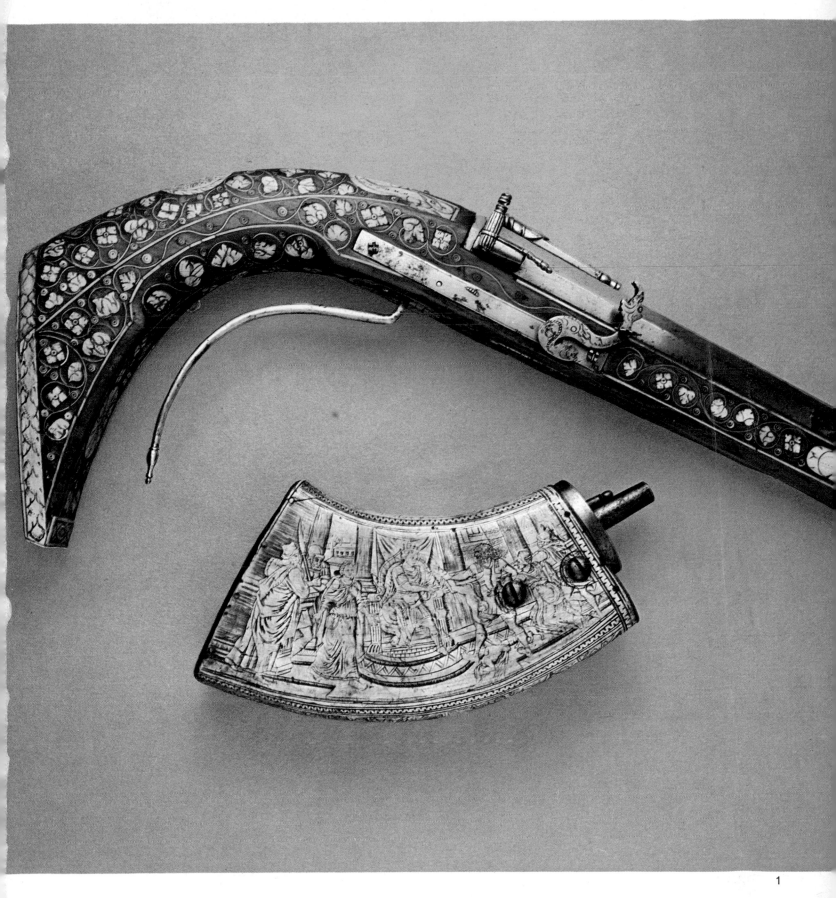

1 Mid sixteenth century petronel (above) and powder flask of the late sixteenth century. The petronel (from the Latin *pectus/pectoris* = chest) was a short arquebus which had to be held against the chest rather than the shoulder to be fired: from the strongly hooked and ample butt one can see why. The shape of the butt shown here is typical of this type of firearm. This petronel, probably French, is a *de luxe* model. Its stock has bone inlay engraved with stylized floral motifs, which are reminiscent of florid gothic rather than the renaissance decoration which would be more usual. However, it is not unusual for firearms of the first half of the sixteenth century to carry archaic ornamentation. The lock-plate is still of the most primitive kind; the pan cover is typical of that period. The decorated cylinder above the octagonal barrel is the backsight: looking through the cylinder one could see the target in the indentation on the foresight. This is a hunting piece, although military firearms of the same period were not so different. The horn powder flask is engraved with a scene depicting the judgment of Solomon. The opening through which the powder is poured is regulated by a spring lever.

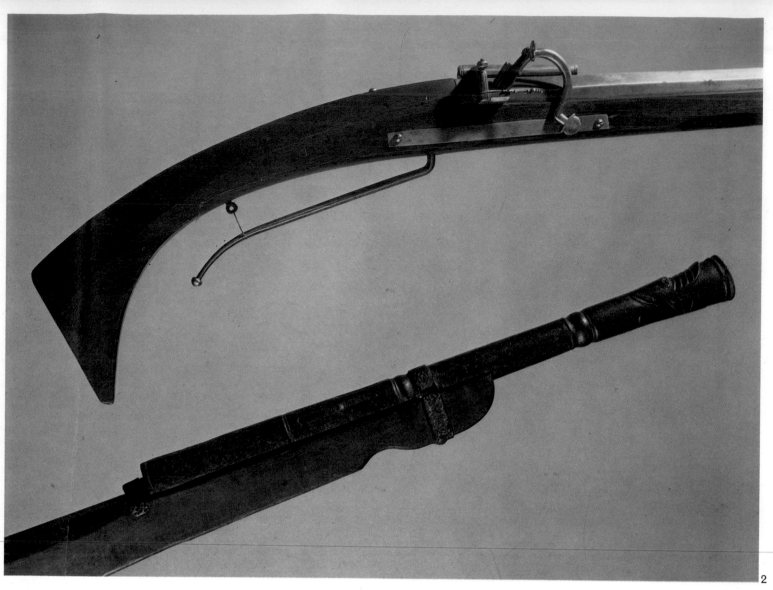

2

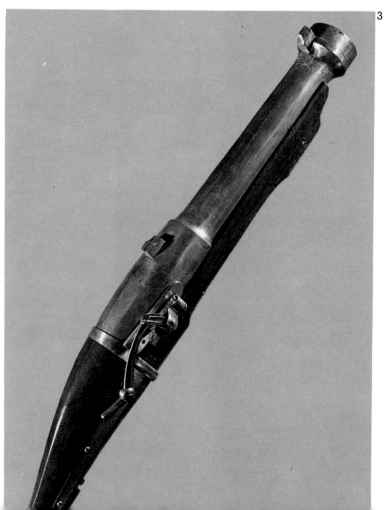

3

2 Sixteenth century match-lock musket (above) and fifteenth century culverin. The latter is mounted on a wooden stock, similar to that of a crossbow, and which has been reconstructed from notes made by Major Angelo Angelucci, one of the greatest Italian antique firearm scholars of the last century. The muzzle of the barrel terminates in a head of a serpent, or culverin. Because of their resemblance to a serpent, guns of medium calibre with very long barrels were given the name of culverin or firemouth. In this portable culverin the flash-pan is still positioned above the breech and has no pan-cover. The arquebus, which probably dates from the second half of the sixteenth century, is a typical military firearm of that period, as is clearly shown by the undecorated wooden stock and the smooth match-plate. As with the petronel shown in the preceding plate, the sear which controls the movement of the serpentine (the curved arm which holds the match) follows the line of the stock. Mechanically the plate is the same as that of the petronel.

3 Portable sixteenth century Japanese culverin. Firearms were introduced into Japan in the sixteenth century by Portuguese and Dutch navigators, who ventured into oriental seas in search of trade. The Japanese mastered these new and dangerous instruments in only a few decades and started to manufacture their own weapons, adapting their shape and usage to their own tastes and technical fancies. Superb craftsmen in bronze, they used this metal for their own firearms which were streamlined, though somewhat bulky and heavy. In the portable culverin shown here the firing system is a Japanese adaptation. It should be mentioned that the screw was then unknown in Japan, and therefore parts were joined by grooving or riveting. This technical ignorance is perhaps the basis of the fact that match-lock firearms were the only type used by the Japanese until the middle of the nineteenth century.

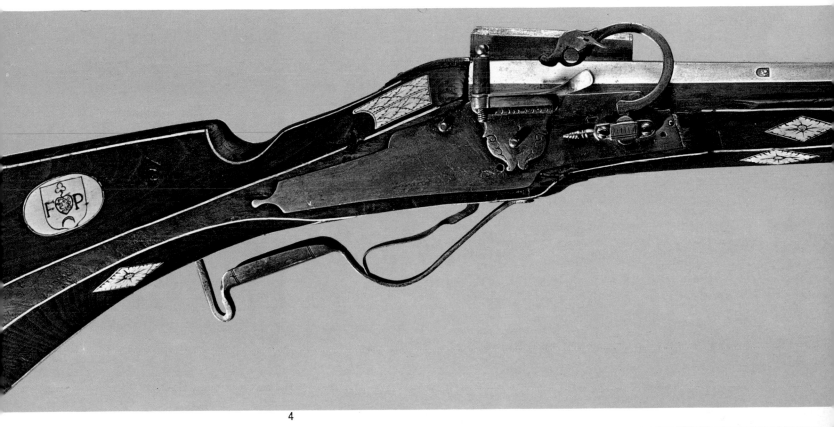

4

4 German match-lock musket with the date 1610 on its barrel. This is a typical military firearm, though beautifully made. It was probably given to the guard by a nobleman. On the oak stock are bone plates, one of which bears the letters F and P, and between these is a heart in which the head of a wild animal is engraved. The lock-plate is of an advanced type and incorporates the pan-cover, as in the flint-lock mechanism. On the barrel (octagonal breech and rounded muzzle) there is a tubular backsight. There is a small sear with a spring lock and a bridge which covers it. The origin of the word 'musket' is uncertain. It came into use in the second half of the sixteenth century, and differs from the arquebus in that it is longer and heavier and has to be fired by resting it on a forked support. The first people to adopt the musket were the Spaniards, during the Flanders campaign. The calibre of this firearm was about 20 millimetres. The shot could pierce armour plate at a distance of 200 metres. It was also the classic infantry weapon during the Thirty Years War.

5 Piedmontese cartridge holder of the seventeenth century. It is made of a bandolier from which are suspended small tubes of boxwood, each containing a charge of powder, and a pouch for carrying shot. These bandoliers were an indispensable part of a musketeer's equipment during this period. The effectiveness of any body of armed men was governed by its ability to fire with the greatest frequency: the charges lying ready to hand allowed this to a greater extent than the horn powder flask.

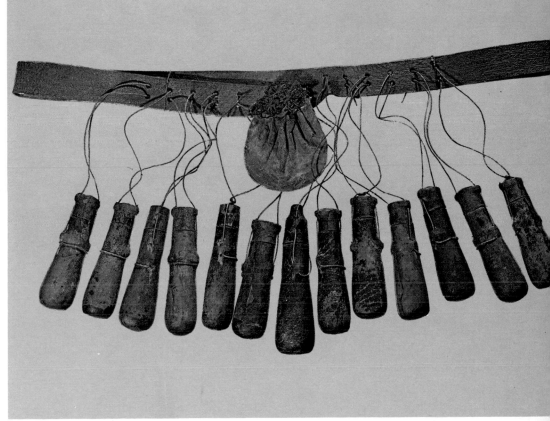

5

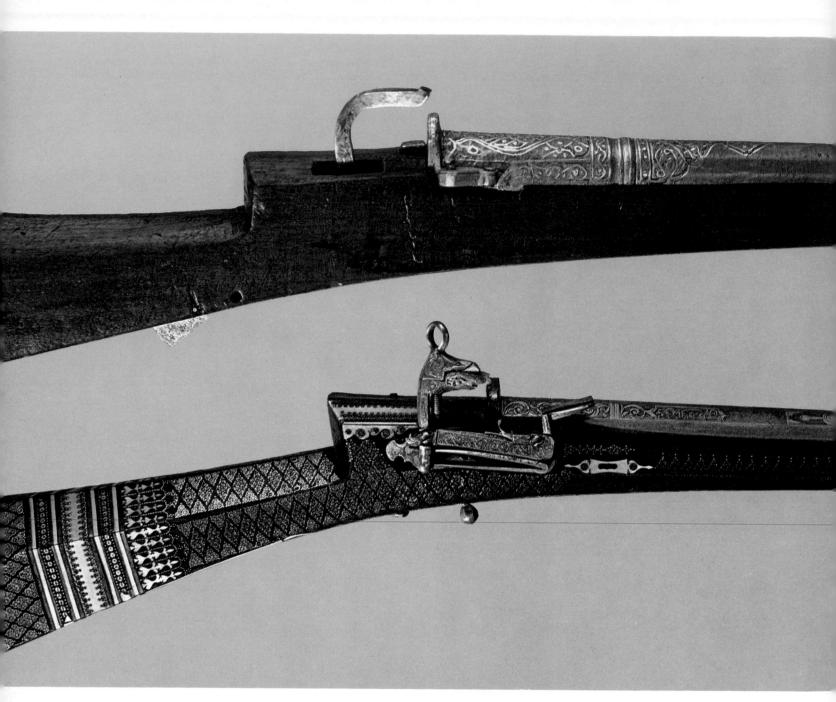

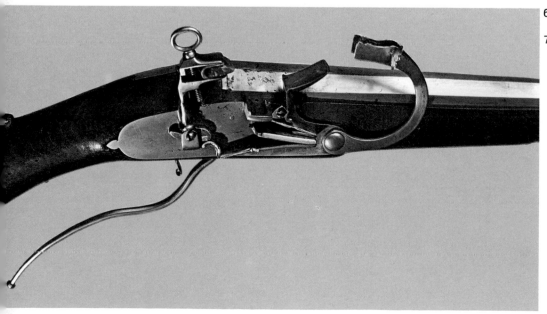

6

7

6 Seventeenth century Turkish match-lock musket (above). The stock is in rustic wood. The barrel is partly decorated with silver inlays, and there is an internal match-lock mechanism. The firearm is typical of those in use in the Near East. In the seventeenth century, armed with the arquebuses, the Ottoman army attempted the last great expansionist thrust towards eastern Europe. The other rifle is a most beautiful example of a Persian firearm, dating from the first half of the nineteenth century. Its shape does not differ from that of the Turkish arquebus of almost two centuries earlier. The stock is richly decorated in bright ivory and brass. The barrel is damascened with gold at the breech and the muzzle. Following Islamic custom, the inlays contain verses from the Koran: Islamic culture has always linked the concept of arms to that of the holy war against the infidel for the glory of Allah and the spreading of his word. The firing mechanism of this rifle is the so-called 'morlacca' type, a version of the Spanish miquelet, made for markets in south east Europe, the Near East and parts of North Africa.

7 Seventeenth century rifle. Frequently the match-lock firing mechanism was combined with the flint-lock or wheel-lock on the same plate, so that either could be fired if the mechanical system mis-fired. That this is a military weapon can be seen from its roughness and utilitarian appearance. The mechanism is a Roman flint-lock (the broken main-spring is badly adjusted and is therefore in the wrong position: it does not in fact engage the lug of the cock, but is underneath, so that the mechanism is completely useless) and match-lock. The sear of the match-lock forms a small bridge for the trigger of the Roman steel.

8 A wheel-lock mechanism dating from the beginning of the seventeenth century. It could be called 'Leonardoesque' since it repeats, with only minimal variations, the wheel shape designed by Leonardo da Vinci in the *Codex Atlanticus*. The wheel is clearly visible together with the square pivot onto which the key is placed when the weapon is cocked. Behind is a shield to prevent the marksman being burnt when the weapon is fired. The link between the wheel and the main-spring is missing. The whole piece is clearly of gothic style and with its curved lines ending sharply it is reminiscent of German firearms. This is a powerful piece, a witness to the ability of the ironsmiths of that time.

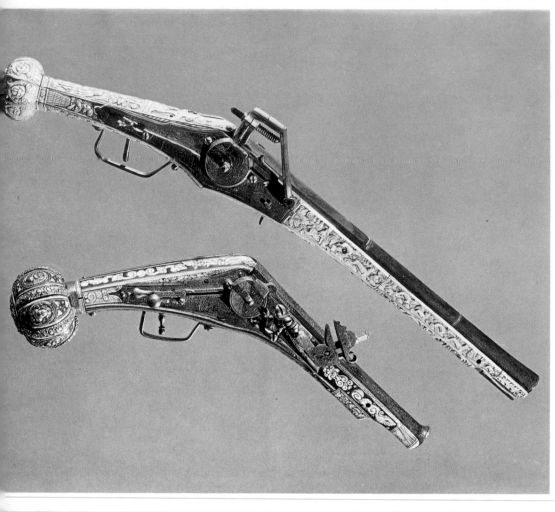

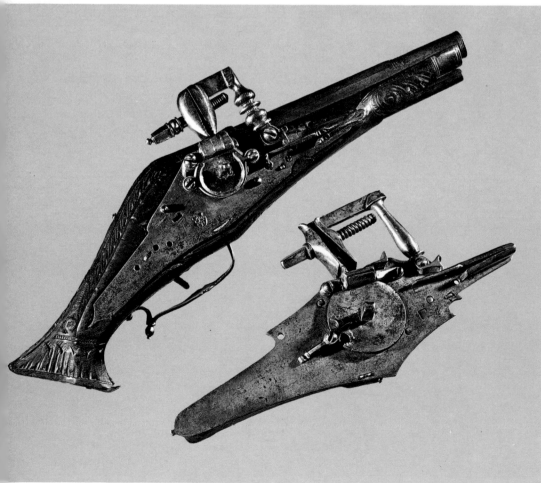

9 Two sixteenth century German pistols. The shape of the top one is almost straight, typical of the firearms of the middle of that century. It was probably made in Saxony. The wheel-lock movement, too, is typical of German production—constructed with heavy plates and without stinting the materials. The wheel is covered and the main-spring is internal. The movement has a safety device. In the plate the cock is pulled down on to the pan cover and is therefore ready for firing. The stock is completely covered with plates of bone carved in high relief with hunting scenes, figures, heads and various ornamentations. The barrel is in two stages, having a round muzzle and octagonal breech. It bears traces of etched decoration, as does the wheel-plate. Its calibre is 14 millimetres. The smaller pistol is also typically German, end of the sixteenth century, and is struck with Nuremberg marks. Wheel-plate and barrel, 24 centimetres long, are decorated with arabesques on a gilded background. The walnut stock is inlaid in horn with ornaments and figures. The angular shape of this piece is peculiar to this type of German pistol. The ball at the end of the stock is made of wood, inlaid with six gilded bronze ribs and six medallions chiselled and gilded. The base of the ball is made of a disc of gilded bronze embossed with a battle scene. The excellence of the work suggests that both these pieces were specially commissioned by noblemen of that period.

10 A pistol and detached lock from Brescia, dating from the second half of the sixteenth century. The pistol dates from about 1570. The barrel is signed Bernardo Paratici; its wheel-plate, however, is German. The stock is made of carved walnut. From this piece one can already observe the tendency of Brescian gunsmiths to create functional pieces: the decorations are simple and reduced to a minimum. The wheel-lock plate from the end of the century has the lozenge form which was to characterise the famous Brescian wheel-locks in the following century.

10

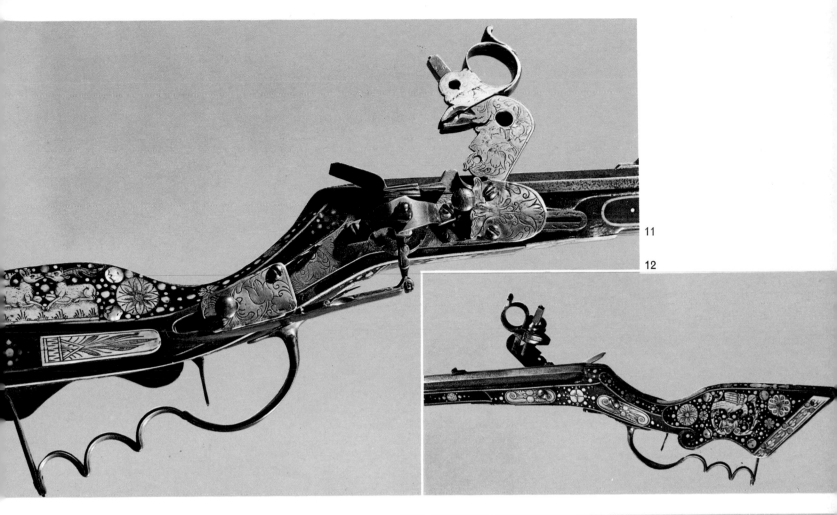

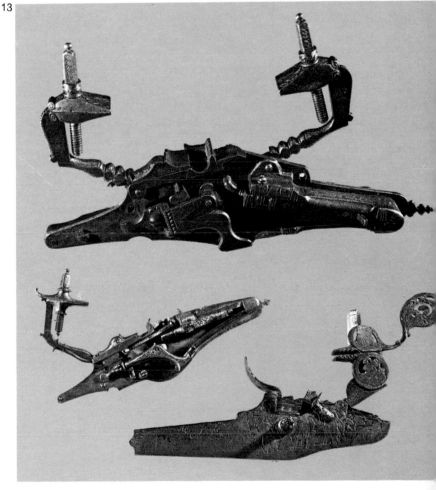

11, 12 A Tschinke from southern Silesia, dating from about 1630. The Tschinke was a small wheel-lock hunting rifle, slender, very light and of small calibre, used throughout the southern German provinces. It began to be produced during the last decades of the sixteenth century and remained in use up to the end of the first quarter of the next century. Apart from those already listed, its principal characteristics were the movement of the covered wheel and the rifled barrel which enabled it to be accurately fired, so that the small bullets had remarkable effect. In practice and without having to make trajectorial calculations, a marksman could hit a hare at 100 metres. It was used for small hunting parties by enthusiasts, beating through the dense forests. The stock of hard wood is richly decorated with inlays of bone and horn depicting animal and floral motifs and pure ornamentation. The plate has been engraved with a burin. The covered wheel has the advantage that the burns caused by the combustion of the powder can be easily cleaned off.

13 Three wheel-lock plates. The first, above, shows the inside and is late sixteenth century, double cocked so that fresh pyrites is always available; it is Farnesian, belonging to that genre of Italian plates which were made for the Farnese family guard. The second, also showing the inside, is a typical Brescian pistol 'rotino', early seventeenth century. The third is Czech, made in Prague towards the middle of the seventeenth century.

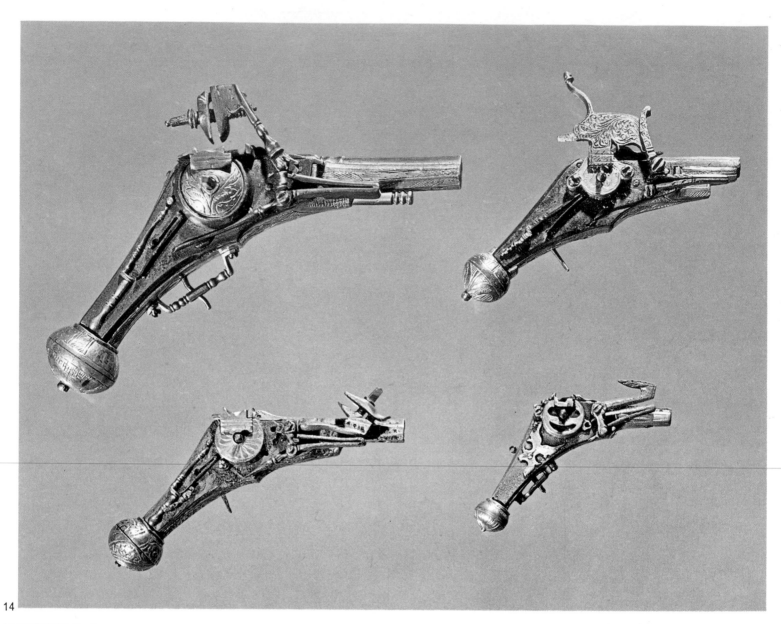

14

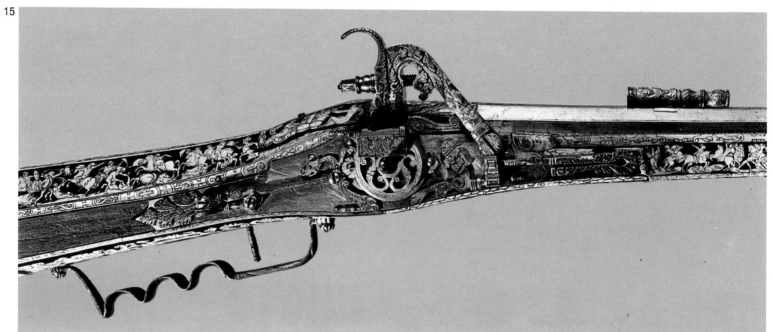

15

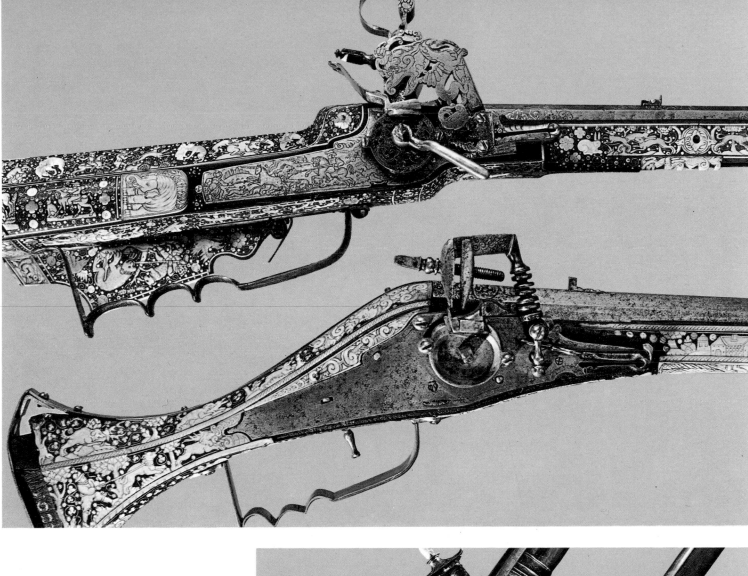

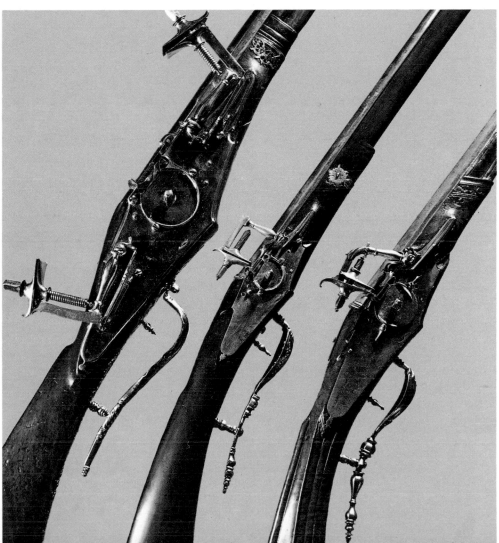

14 'Bijou' match-lock pistols dating from the middle of the sixteenth century. They come from Nuremberg and are examples of the skill possessed by the mechanics of this German city, the centre of production of firearms and precision mechanisms such as watches. These pistols are shown slightly magnified; they still function perfectly. They were often worn by officers in town guards.

15 German wheel-lock arquebus dating from the end of the sixteenth century. It carries the marking of Ausburg, another large centre producing firearms. Lock, stock and barrel are richly decorated. Scenes of classical warriors, clearly of renaissance style, are inlaid in bone on the wooden stock. Gilded classical warriors in low relief decorate the barrel at the breech, half way along and at the muzzle. The backsight is gilded, as is the etched lock-plate: altogether a most beautiful and aristocratic hunting piece.

16 Two German hunting wheel-lock arquebuses. The one above is richly decorated with mother-of-pearl inlays and plates of bone on the stock. Hunting scenes, animals, and stylized flowers are depicted. The wheel-plate with its Silesian-type cock is also engraved with stylized hunting motifs. The key is placed upon the pivot of the wheel. The other arquebus also dates from the early seventeenth century. The stock carries inlaid hunting scenes and animals; it has a plain lock and barrel.

17 Three Brescian wheel-lock guns. The two on the left date from the end of the sixteenth century, and were used by mounted carabiniers. The third is early seventeenth century.

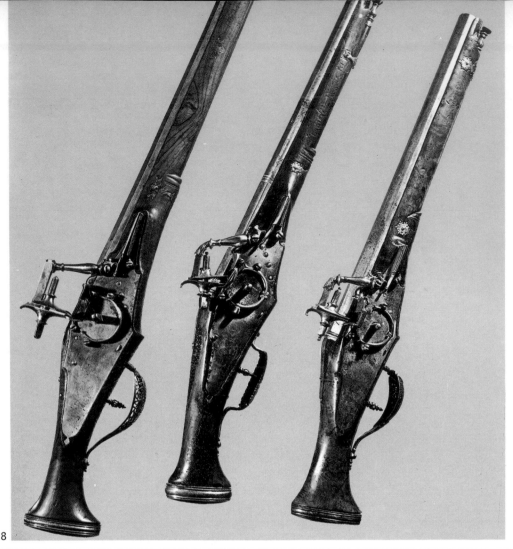

18

18 Three Brescian wheel-lock pistols. If the Germans were the best makers of wheel-lock firearms (this firing system remained in use with them right up to the beginning of the eighteenth century, although not as widely diffused as in the sixteenth and seventeenth centuries), Brescian gunsmiths—who flourished in the Val Trompia—were the second best. And while German wheel-lock firearms were always rather heavy, very bulky and frequently over-decorated, the Brescian version was distinguished by precisely the opposite characteristics: lightness, compactness, and elegant but sober decoration. The Brescian 'rotino', the wheel-lock mechanism made by their craftsmen, was justly famous and sought after for its lightness and convenience; as were the barrels, long, of small calibre and extremely light although very strong. These three pistols are typically Brescian in form and construction. That on the left dates from the end of the sixteenth century, has a walnut stock, a slender wheel-plate, and a trigger guard in pierced iron. The angled cock is of sixteenth century design. The second dates from the beginning of the seventeenth century with a stock in decorated walnut, which instead of being pierced is ornamented with small nails. The third pistol has a butt in brierwood and dates from the beginning of the seventeenth century. Here too, decoration is reduced to a minimum. Note the almost straight butt of these three pistols and the absence of foresights. In fact these pistols are made to be fired quickly, over short distances.

19 Brescian wheel-lock pistol dating from the first half of the seventeenth century, which we could call a pocket pistol on account of its compactness. The shape of this piece differs from the classic Brescian line by the type of plate which is not of the lozenge shape favoured by the craftsmen of the Val Trompia. In fact the decorations on the plate are in the French style (in gold on the barrel, plate and on the fittings—the bridge and the butt plate). It can be assumed therefore that this piece was made for export. The Brescian arms industry was in fact so advanced that its products were sought abroad. It should be observed, however, that both the wheel and the cock are of the standard Brescian type and only the shape of the plate itself, on which the mechanism is mounted, is of French type.

19

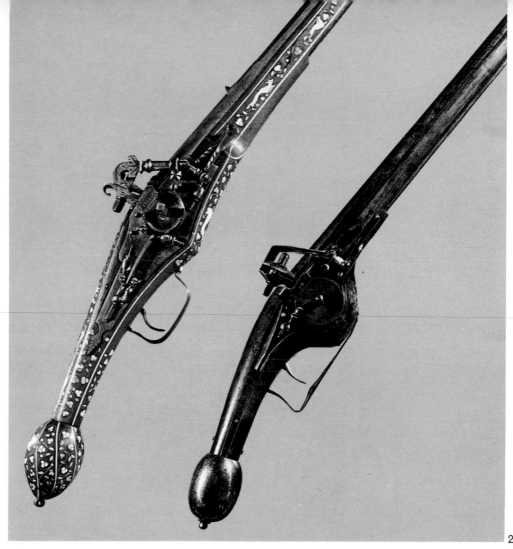

20 Two holster pistols dating from the beginning of the seventeenth century. They are cavalry arms, with long barrels. They reflect the characteristics of a type of pistol with a lemon butt, very similar to the apple of the sword hilts of that period. The apple made the grip on the butt more secure. In general these pistols were carried in pairs, so that horsemen could fire twice in succession. The piece on the left is German, dated 1619. The butt in pearwood is inlaid with floral motifs in ivory. The spiral decoration on the stock is very elegant. The other pistol is French with a polished stock and apple butt. Neither wheel-plate nor barrel are decorated. The French wheel-plate differs from the German and Brescian ones, for the internal main-spring has been extended along the stock.

21 A pair of German wheel-lock pistols from the Thirty Years War period (1618–1648). During this long period the struggles involved nearly all the European nations and the demand for arms increased enormously. From this arises the fact that although well made, military arms of this period are seldom over-decorated. The pistols shown here have, however, one characteristic in common: they are 'automatic', i.e. the wheel charges by raising and lowering the cock without recourse to the usual key.

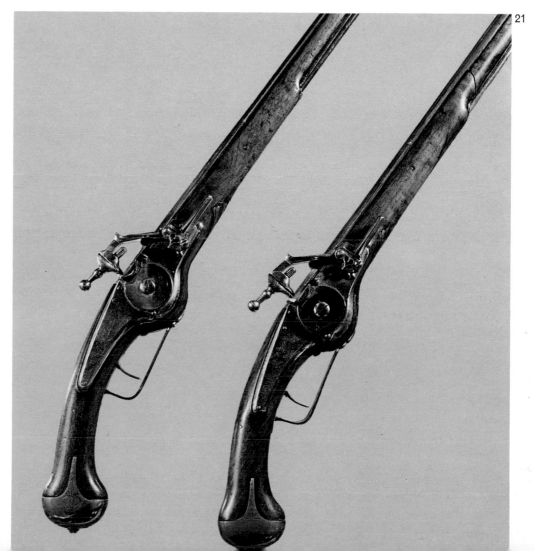

22 Series of accessories for wheel-lock firearms. From the left: a combination wheel-key, screwdriver and priming flask, German late sixteenth century; a combination powder flask and shot-pouch (above), late sixteenth century, for use with a Tschinke; and a circular German powder flask. The first is in wood with mother-of-pearl inlay, while the second is decorated with the bone inlay which is typical of this type of accessory in the first half of the seventeenth century. Combination tools with key, screwdriver and powder-holder for primer, similar to those at the top and first on the right; lastly, a powder-horn in wood and iron, with bone inlay, dating from the end of the sixteenth century, and bearing the marks of Nuremberg.

23 From the left: a horn wheel-key of the end of the seventeenth century or beginning of the eighteenth century; a set of wheel-key, screwdriver and horn powder-holder of the early eighteenth century; powder-flask of the end of the eighteenth century; horn powder-holder of the end of the eighteenth century; powder-flask of the early eighteenth century carved out of a defective antler. These accessories are German and Austrian, and show the continuing use of wheel-lock firearms in Germany and Austria as the favourite hunting weapons.

24 Neapolitan or Brescian 'miquelet' flint-lock with double firing mechanism, second half of the seventeenth century, and Portuguese 'miquelet' flint-lock. The 'miquelet' and the Roman flint-lock could also be termed 'Mediterranean flint-locks' as they were in use, albeit with slight variations in shape, throughout the Mediterranean countries, including Portugal which felt the influence of her neighbour, Spain. As far as Italy was concerned, in her large production of firearms she could not afford to ignore Spanish taste, for two simple reasons: Spain was an excellent client, and moreover had political supremacy over the South (Neapolitan gunsmiths) and in Lombardy (Brescian gunsmiths). Consequently, alongside original firing systems like the Roman flint-lock and the Italian snaphaunce, there was also an Italian version of the Spanish 'miquelet'. This was mechanically similar to that produced by Spanish craftsmen, but was distinguished by the richness of the ornamentation. The Italian craftsmen, and especially those from the region of Brescia, experts in working with iron, indulged their whims in creating flint-locks. This is evident in this double-firing mechanism, in which all the parts including the spring were decorated in relief, even full relief, after the Baroque taste of the period. This plate was made for a double-barrelled gun or for a gun with a double touch-hole to the barrel, to be loaded with superimposed charges. In the second example, the front lock would be fired first, then the other. The Portuguese flint-lock, below, is early eighteenth century and is seen from the inside. Note the simplicity of the parts which make up the firing mechanism.

24

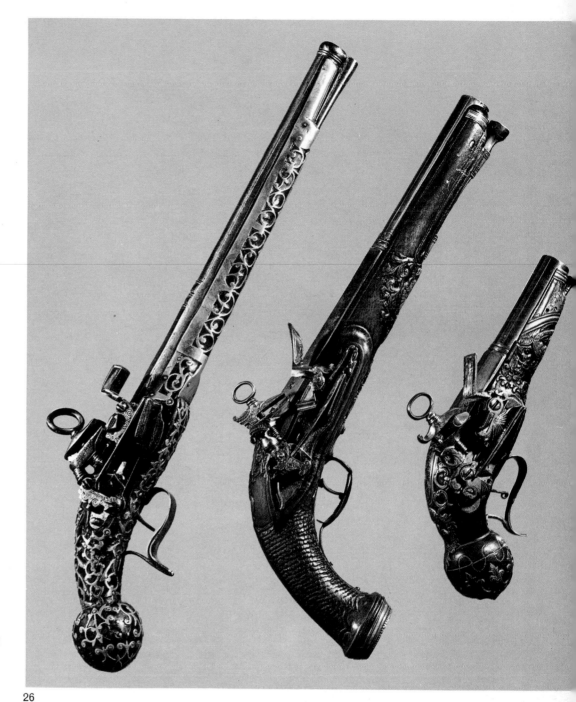

25 Three Spanish pistols of the kind made at Ripoll, one of the most renowned centres for firearms in Spain. That on the left has the classic rounded butt of that locality; it dates from the second half of the seventeenth century and the stock is decorated with silver inlay. The second has the stock entirely covered with brass, and dates from the beginning of the eighteenth century. The third, with its stock decorated with silver, also dates from the beginning of the eighteenth century. All three are equipped with 'miquelet' flint-locks of the classic kind. The first and the third have barrels with a counterpoise weight at the muzzle, similar to those made by the Italians of Brescia which were so fashionable.

26 Three pistols with 'miquelet' flint-lock. The first is Spanish, from Ripoll, and dates from the middle of the seventeenth century; the stock is decorated with brass inlay in the characteristic style of weapons from Ripoll. The second is Neapolitan, from the end of the eighteenth century; the stock is walnut with silver decoration. The third, dating from the last years of the seventeenth century, is also Neapolitan, although it is in the Ripoll style; it is a sturdy pocket pistol which could be lethal at close range. The mechanisms of these three weapons, though made at different places and times, are identical, and give evidence of the lasting appreciation of this simple and sound mechanism.

26

27 A Tuscan rifle of the second half of the seventeenth century, with Roman flint-lock. It is decorated in silver and bears on the barrel the marks of the Medici Arsenal. The lock-plate on which the mechanism is mounted is the same shape as that of a flint-lock, i.e. with an internal spring. Note that the spring is not operated by the rear foot of the cock from below upwards, as in the 'miquelet', but by the forward foot, from above downwards.

27

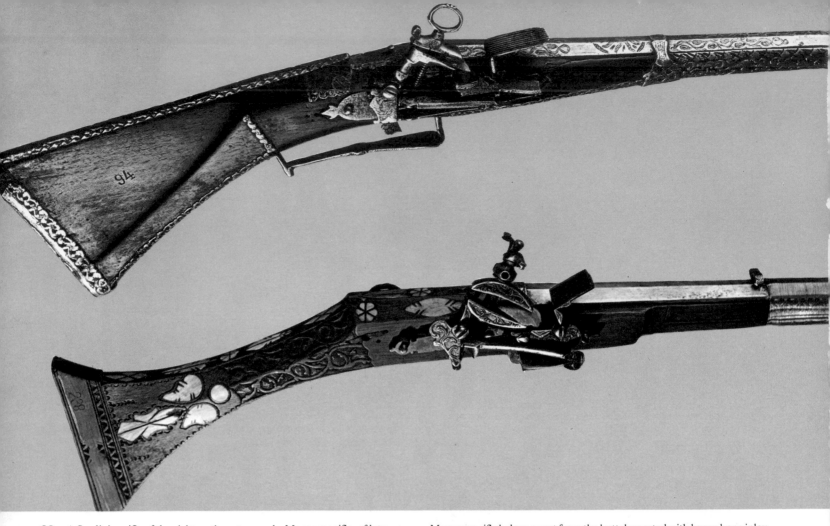

28 A Sardinian rifle of the eighteenth century and a Moroccan rifle, of late eighteenth or early nineteenth century. The Sardinian rifle is distinguished by its own special characteristics, and above all by its shape. In its long barrel (from 120 to 140 centimetres) which is also slender and of small calibre (10 to 12 millimetres); and in its fin-shaped butt, the Sardinian rifle follows the Mediterranean tradition of the extremely light and portable rifle, with a flat trajectory, and precision even at notable distances. The butt is a modification of those of the Lombard arquebuses of the second half of the sixteenth century: on the stock a triangular addition has been attached to the upper, straightened surface, which facilitates the resting of the cheek here while firing; the forestock is separate from the butt, and overlaid with plates of brass, iron and silver. The Sardinian rifle is often decorated to a greater or a lesser degree, over the salients of the wooden butt. The flint-lock is of the 'miquelet' type, sometimes the Roman version. As it was not possible to manufacture the barrels and flint-locks in the island, these were imported, especially from the region of Brescia; and from the middle of the eighteenth century, also from Naples. The locks and barrels were imported in the rough state, and the final ornamentation was entrusted to the gunsmiths of the island, among whom the name of one craftsman appears more frequently than any other: Barbuti. In the

Moroccan rifle below, apart from the butt decorated with heavy bone inlay, note the particular version of the 'miquelet' flint-lock made for export to North African countries.

29–30 Cossack pistols with 'Moldo-Wallachian' flint-lock and a 'Moldo-Wallachian' flint-lock for an arquebus. This type of flint-lock was produced in Italy for export to eastern Europe, the Balkans as far as southern Russia, and Turkey. In reality it was a 'miquelet' in which a plate, called an apron, joined the pivot of the steel with that of the cock. Its function was to cover partly or wholly the spring, and to render more sturdy the combination of parts in the lock. The Cossack pistol is distinguished by its long, thin barrel, and by its angled grip, completed by a substantial pommel (knob). In plate 29, the upper pistol has a wooden stock covered in leather, and an ivory pommel; the stock of the other is covered in gilded and silvered brass, richly ornamented. In plate 30 the stock of the pistol is made of horn and the pommel of ivory. The three pistols all date from the beginning of the nineteenth century. The large arquebus flintlock in plate 30 dates from the end of the eighteenth century, and is decorated with voluted motifs and semi-precious stones set in the apron.

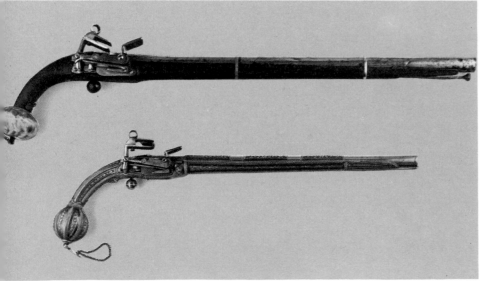

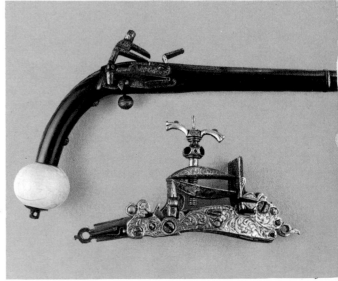

29   30

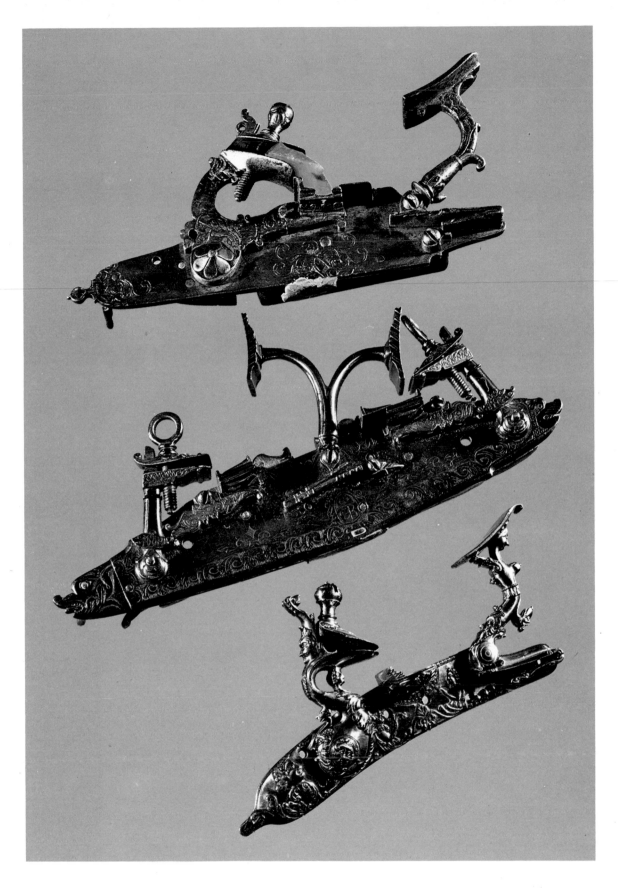

31   From the top: a Brescian snaphaunce (or 'Florentine') flint-lock of the early seventeenth century; a snaphaunce flint-lock with two opposite steels, probably Brescian of the beginning of the seventeenth century; a Tuscan snaphaunce flint-lock of the eighteenth century. The Italian snaphaunce can be differentiated from those of northern Europe by their constant elegance of execution. Neat, light, and well made, the snaphaunce of Tuscany and Emilia, called the 'Florentine' snaphaunce, was never used as a flint-lock of war. This was precluded by its intrinsic fragility, in comparison with the flint-lock type in which the combined unit of the steel and the cap-cover offered greater strength. The first of the locks shown in this plate has certain archaic characteristics in the straight shape of the lock-plate, in the arm of the steel, and the squared shoes of the cock; but the second is decidedly archaic, with its erect cocks similar to those of a 'miquelet'. This piece is interesting also because of the mechanism devised in the double-firing flint-lock with opposite steels, mounted on a single stem. It was probably made for a rifle with a single barrel, to be loaded with superimposed charges. The third is in the purer eighteenth century tradition of Anghiari, and is signed Brenta.

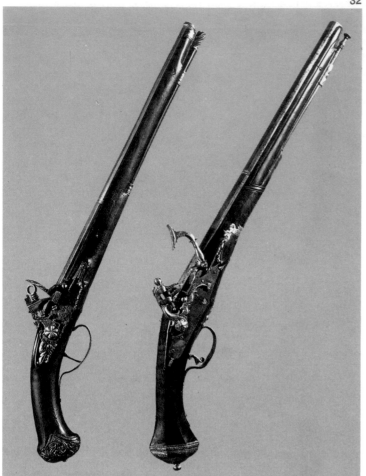

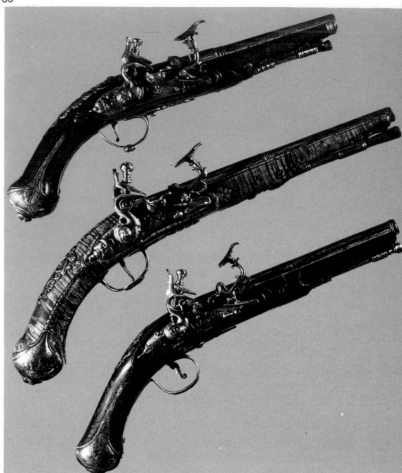

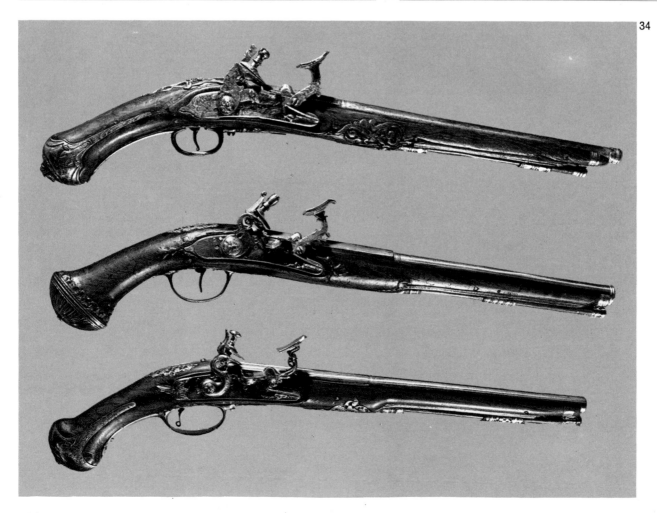

34

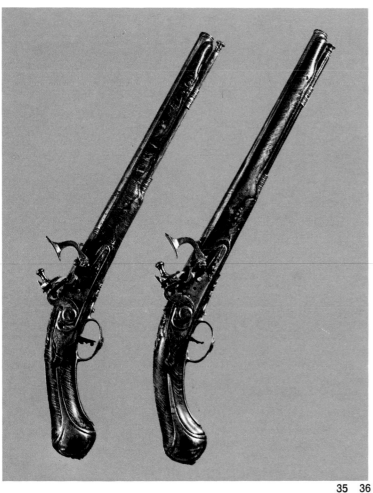

35 36

35 A pair of Brescian holster pistols with snaphaunce locks, dating from the second half of the seventeenth century and signed Antonio Franzino. The holster, or cavalry, pistols were placed in roomy sheaths at the side of the saddles. They could reach a length of 50 centimetres and were dangerous at a range of more than 50 metres. The stocks are of walnut root with the usual elegant iron furnishings.

36 From the top: a pair of Tuscan snaphaunce pistols, signed Bracciolini and dating from the middle of the eighteenth century. The barrels bear the marks of the Medici Arsenal. The second pair are child's pistols made by the important Anghiari gunsmith Domenico Guardiani, who was working in the second half of the eighteenth century.

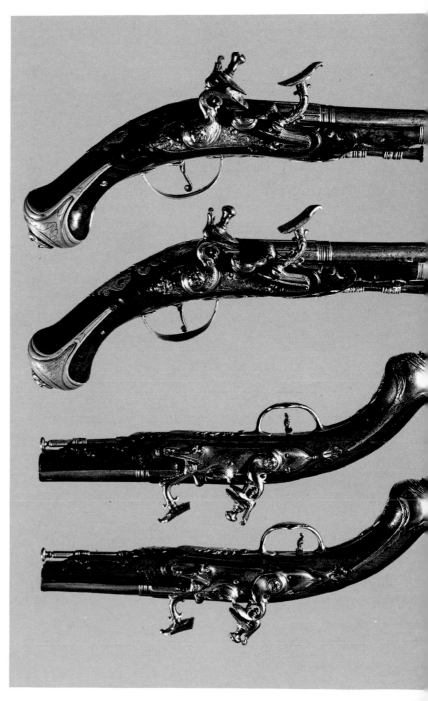

32 Brescian pistols with the 'Florentine' flint-lock. Both have barrels signed by members of the Cominazzo family, the most celebrated barrel makers of the Val Trompia. The one on the right, the barrel of which is signed Vicenzo Cominazzo, dates from the early years of the seventeenth century; the butt is walnut with decorations of metal filigree; the lock is of archaic form. The second example, signed Domenico Lazzarino, dates from the earliest years of the seventeenth century, and reflects the shapes of the butt and plate which were fashionable at the time for wheel-lock pistols.

33 From the top: a Brescian snaphaunce pistol of the end of the seventeenth century; it has a walnut butt with steel mounts, and the lock-plate is decorated with medallions, a widely used ornament for this type of weapon. An Italian snaphaunce pistol of the beginning of the eighteenth century; the butt is in elegant walnut root with worked iron furnishings. Lastly, an eighteenth century snaphaunce pistol of Anghiari, signed by Giuseppe Guardiani, who was one of the most noted of a celebrated family of gunsmiths of Anghiari.

34 Three long snaphaunce pistols from Italy. The one at the top dates from the first half of the eighteenth century; the furnishings of the butt are in worked iron. The second one is also of the same period and is signed Corsini. The third is from Brescia, from the end of the seventeenth century; it is decorated with the iron filigree work which is typical of Brescian products of good quality.

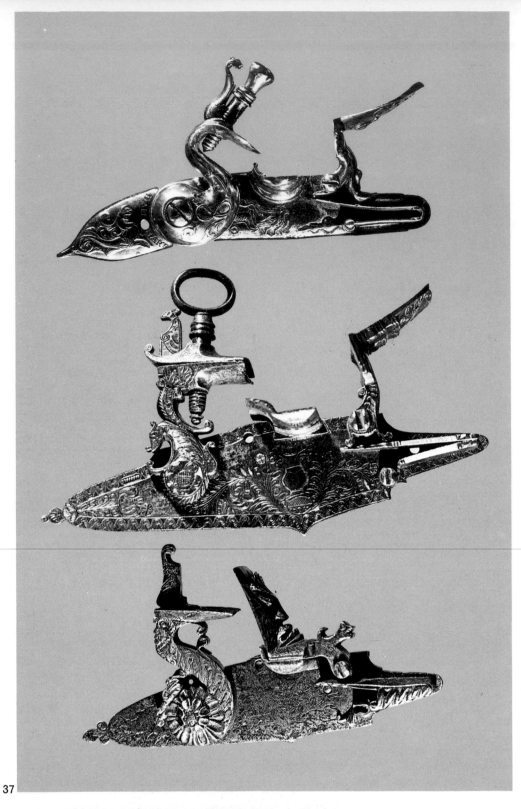

37 Three detached flint-lock mechanisms. The first two are shown with the steels and pan covers raised; in the bottom it is in the firing position. At the top is a typical flint-lock of the middle eighteenth century, having a slightly curved lock-plate of blunted shape. It has an internal mainspring, and the plate is engraved all over. The upper jaw of the cock is missing. The middle one is Brescian, of the first half of the seventeenth century, and, like the snaphaunces of the same period, it is still archaic in the rhomboid shape of the plate, reminiscent of those in wheel-lock pistols. It is richly decorated with engraving and low relief. The third is also Brescian, and dates from the first half of the seventeenth century. The upper jaw of the cock is missing.

38 A Brescian pistol of about 1660, signed Garatto. In its neat and graceful shape it is a forerunner of the style of pistols for almost the whole of the next century. The furnishings are in iron, elegantly worked, and the lock is fitted with a swan-neck hammer.

39 A pair of Brescian pistols with the barrels signed Lazarino Cominazzo, dating from the first half of the seventeenth century. The furnishings and the locks bear the signature of one of the most renowned Brescian engravers of the time: Andrea Pizzi. It is to be noted that in luxury firearms from Brescia everything made of iron is decorated with engraving, with chiselled relief, or with free-standing ornament, including the trigger. On the other hand, in other European countries including France and Austria, where the stock, barrel and mounts of firearms were all subject to veritable orgies of Baroque and Rococo ornament, the trigger was always a smooth part, at the most ending in a volute.

40 Two pistols, one French (on the left) and the other Italian, both of the seventeenth century. The French pistol has two barrels made of brass, and is of small calibre; the charges are fired by a single striking mechanism. The furnishings are in bronze, including the lock-plate. The cock, steel and internal parts only are in steel. It is clearly a firearm made for someone who had to go to sea, and is therefore made of materials which are not corroded by salt. The Italian pistol is from Brescia and signed Lazarino Cominazzo. The butt is in walnut decorated with pierced steel fittings. Even the trigger is worked in the round; note that in the French weapon this part is smooth.

37

38

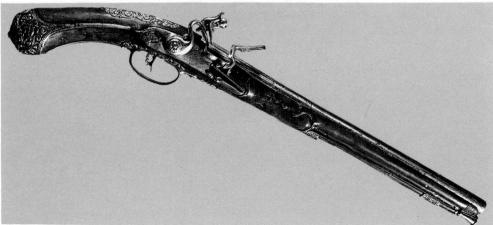

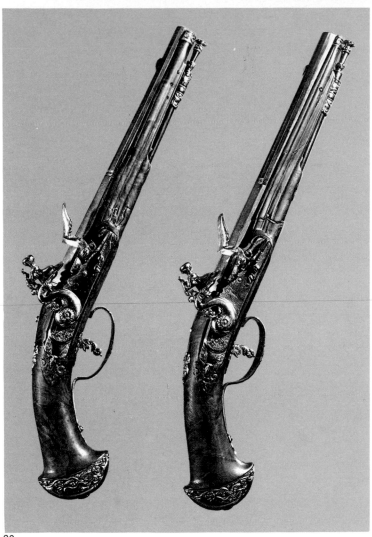

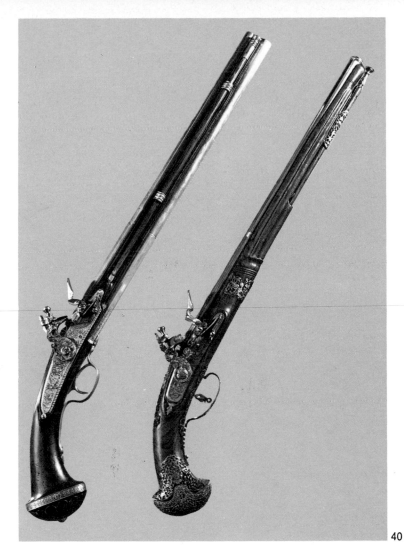

39

40

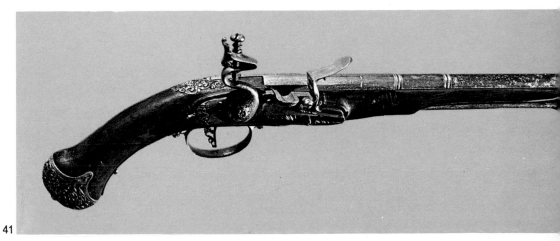

41

42

41 A Brescian flint-lock pistol, about 1670. The barrel is signed Lazarino Cominazzo; the lock-plate carries the signature of Tonino Borgognone – Brescia. The barrel in two stages has octagonal breech and rounded muzzle; the furnishings are in chiselled steel.

42 Austrian pistol of about 1630 in the style of Hans Schmidt of Ferlach, an excellent gunsmith of the first half of the seventeenth century. It was originally a wheel-lock pistol, as is clearly indicated both by the straight stock and the swelling beneath, which held the round form of the wheel-plate. It was modified to take a flint, probably in the second half of the century, by cutting the wheel-plate and inserting the lock. The barrel is in two stages, and the stock displays fine silver inlay and iron furnishings.

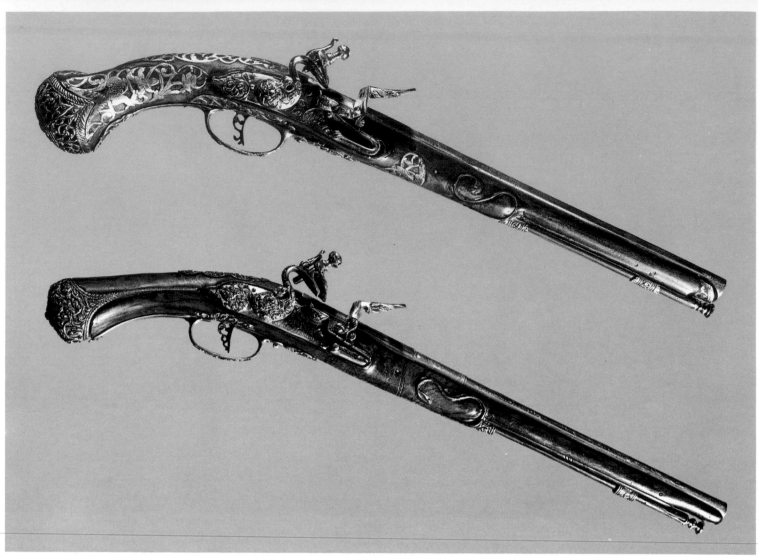

43 Two Brescian pistols, the top one dating from the late seventeenth century, the other of 1660–1670. In the second example the barrel is signed Bonomini, the stock is straight and ends in a slight enlargement. The furnishings are of chiselled iron. In the first, although the flint-lock is elegantly worked, the stock is covered with somewhat coarse pierced iron plates, reminiscent of the pistols of Ripoll.

44 On the left: a magnificent Roman pistol of the first half of the eighteenth century. The barrel is burnished and inlaid with silver, and the furnishings are in gilded brass with silver medallions. It bears the coat of arms of the Orsini family. The second, dating from the second half of the eighteenth century, is Brescian and was made by Giuseppe Merli; the butt is of root walnut decorated with silver wire, and the furniture is also of silver. The shape of these pistols is typical of the late seventeenth century and remained in fashion for about one hundred years. In these two pistols note the French influence in the decoration, which is rich and rather showy, especially in the Orsini pistol.

45 Two blunderbusses and a short carbine, all with hinged folding butts, Brescian, eighteenth century. The one on the left is signed Lazzaro Lazzarini; its stock in root walnut has silver inlay, and it dates from about 1740. The second is a very fine weapon of the end of the eighteenth century, with the butt in root walnut, decorated in silver, and with a gilded pan to prevent corrosion. It is signed Beccalossi in Brescia, and the excellence of its construction indicates clearly that at the end of the eighteenth century the Brescian gunsmithing tradition still had extremely able exponents. The third weapon is a beautifully made short carbine of the end of the seventeenth century, signed Garatto. This, like the other two, has a folding stock. This is a characteristic of firearms made for travelling, and needless to say for brigandry and ambushes. With the stock folded, they could be hidden under a cloak and were more easily carried without being noticed. The two blunderbusses are typical weapons of defence at short range. Loaded with large grape-shot, they discharged a shower of projectiles which hit the mark even in a hurry. The blunderbuss was also extremely useful against an enemy who had reached the moat or ditch surrounding a fortification. Originally brought into use in the seventeenth century, it remained a civil and a military weapon until half-way through the nineteenth century, even though nowadays it is recognized that its funnel-shaped barrel did not affect the dispersal of the shot. However, this kind of splayed barrel allowed rapid loading from the muzzle end. The Beccalossi blunderbuss in the photograph is also armed with a long bayonet which, when freed from a special catch, would spring forward; the shot having been fired, it was always possible to rely on this blade in continuing the defence.

46 Turkish Empire blunderbuss-pistol, of the eighteenth century. The locks were usually of European design and manufacture, as was often the whole weapon, to which decorations in line with oriental taste were added, especially on the barrel. The special shape of the stock, resembling a gun-butt, allowed the weapon to be fired from the hip or the knee, to absorb the heavy recoil.

47 French percussion cap double-barrelled over-and-under blunderbuss-pistol, with flattened oval bell mouth, about 1830, signed Le Page à Paris: percussion system with nipple. Le Page, an excellent Parisian gunmaker, was still making bell-mouthed arms in 1830. The flattened bell mouth was no doubt intended to give a wider horizontal field, but it is not certain that the method gave the desired results. Note the excellent browning of the barrels, which bear the maker's name in gold, in an oval panel. The locks are of back action type.

45

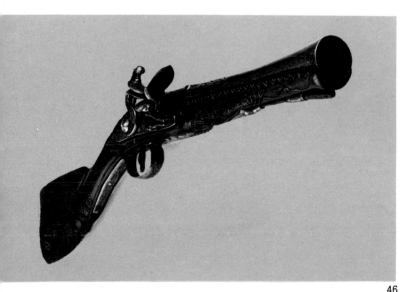

46

47

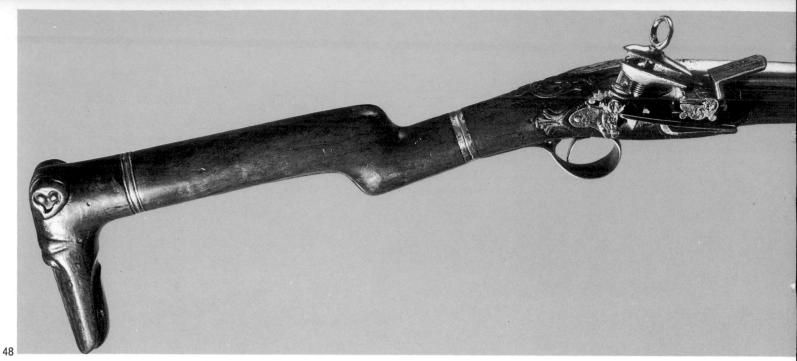

48

49

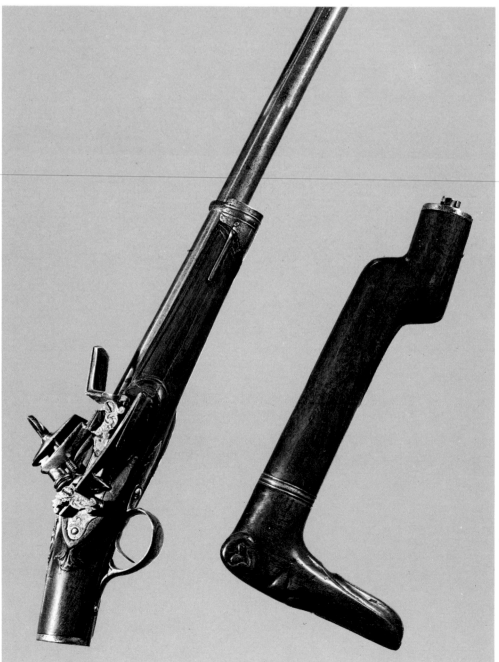

48-49 Spanish traveller's gun of the middle
eighteenth century in the form of a stick (plate 48)
which can be broken down into two parts (plate 49).
It is signed Bustindui, the name of several good
gunmakers of the eighteenth century who worked
in the armament centre of Eibar. Like the short
bell-mouthed pistols on the preceding page, it
belonged to the class of secret arms. The device by
which it could be broken down into two parts made
it easily hidden: moreover, even when assembled,
it might pass as an ordinary walking stick if the
barrel and lock were covered by the owner's
cloak. The lock is of the 'miquelet' type in its more

classic form. The weapon is a true gun, though with a shorter barrel and a smaller bore than those generally in use at that time.

50 Pocket pistol with dagger-type butt, of the seventeenth century. This too is a secret weapon. Carried in the belt, it would pass for a sword or dagger because of the form of the butt: but it was actually an efficient flint-lock pistol. In fact, it was not uncommon for true steel weapons (daggers, sabres, and large knives) to be fitted with a barrel and lock alongside the blade, thus giving the advantages of both types of weapon.

52

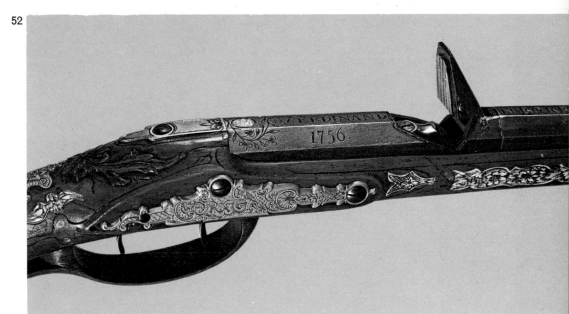

51 Tuscan flint-lock gun of the second half of the seventeenth century, signed Lorenzoni. He was one of the most famous gunmakers of his time, whose products were highly esteemed by Cosimo de' Medici III, Grand Duke of Tuscany. Michele Lorenzoni was not only a gunmaker, though he was one of the best of the craft: his work was characterized by inventive genius, as in this case; the gun, similar to so many other valuable arms of the period in shape and decoration, has in addition a special safety action. The lower part of the pan cover consists of a small steel plate hinged to the horizontal underside of the cover. This device made it possible to keep the hammer at full cock, without risk of accidental discharge, as the pan was covered. To fire, it was only necessary to lower the steel, which was then still coupled to the plate below it, forming a single block which rose on the impact of the cock, uncovering the opening of the pan as in all flint-lock guns. The photo shows clearly the pan covering plate, half-lifted and separate from the steel.

52 Bohemian gun, with waterproof flint-lock action, dated 1756 by Ferdinand Moraveck of Bokrumau. The action is of the internal flint type. The flint is fixed to a plunger, the stem of which moved inside a coiled spring. The lock was cocked with a small lever on the left side of the gun, which held the plunger on its seat behind the breech, with the spring compressed. The hammer consisted of an extension of the breech, triangular in section, hinged, and held down by a spring. When the cock was lowered, it formed a single unit with the breech extension in which was formed the cylindrical seating for the plunger holding the flint: the weapon was then free from any projection. Under the hammer is the pan, the vent being in the back of the breech. When the trigger was pressed, the seat of the plunger-cock was released and the spring drove the flint sharply against the hammer, which, when closed, had an angular internal surface. The sparks resulting from the impact fell into the pan and fired the charge. The waterproof character of the action is chiefly due to the excellent workmanship of the steel and its seating.

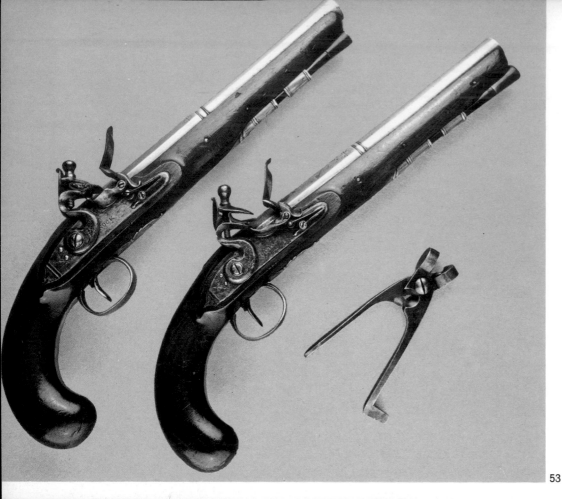

53

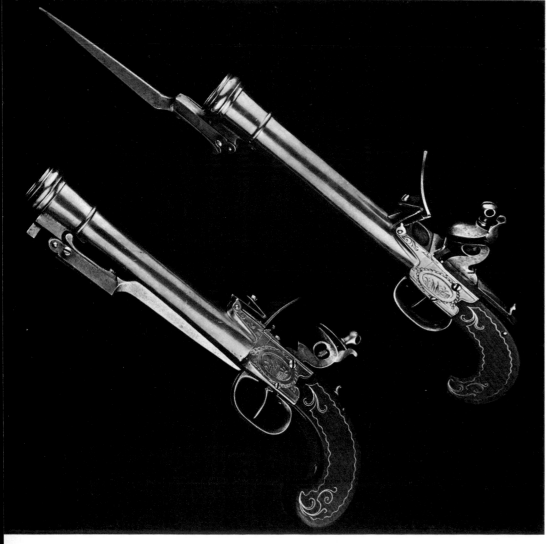

54

53 Pair of eighteenth century British naval officer's flint-lock pistols. Beside them is a bullet-mould of the same period. These are by Henry Nock, a gunmaker who was active in London and Birmingham from 1760 to 1810, and was famous for both civilian and military arms. He carried out several large government contracts. This pair of pistols have brass barrels and fittings to prevent corrosion by sea air. English weapons at the end of the eighteenth century are characteristically functional, as is shown in these pistols by the convenient angle of the butt and the high quality of the barrels and mechanical parts.

54 Pair of French naval pistols, with brass barrels, folding bayonets and box locks, of the late eighteenth or early nineteenth century. The barrels are slightly bell-mouthed to make loading easier in difficult conditions. The folding bayonet is thrown into position by a spring when the trigger guard is drawn back, the point of the bayonet being housed in the front of the guard. The flint-lock action is of the box type, being contained in a metal housing in line with the barrel. The walnut butt, in this case decorated with a modest silver inlay, is of the form called 'bird's head'. The weapon can be made safe by pushing forward a steel plate which enters a notch in the base of the steel: this can be seen in the pistol on the right.

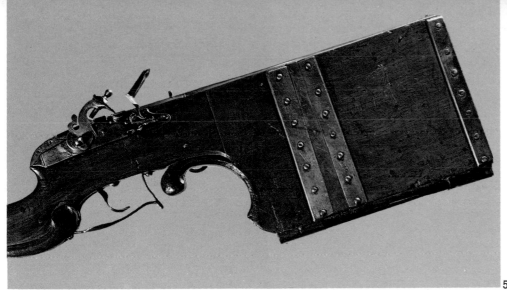

56

57

55 'Battle-organ' of the seventeenth century. This is a heavy thirteen-barrelled pistol (hence the name of 'organ'), all barrels being fired by a single lock. The effect was like that of a blast of grape-shot. As it was practically impossible to withstand the recoil of such a discharge, the arm was hooked over a wall or stake by the bracket below.

56 French military flint-lock musket, 1777 model. That backbone of the army, the infantry, was armed with long muskets (about 1.30 metres in length) the bore of which varied from 16 to 18 milli-metres. A bayonet of triangular section could be fixed to the weapon by means of a socket which slipped over the end of the barrel. The arms factories of various countries made a type of musket which differed little from one country to another. The most carefully-made part was naturally the lock, with a strong double-necked cock. The Napoleonic wars were fought with such muskets. The effective range of the arm was about three hundred metres; the probability of hitting a target was already very small at one hundred metres. In defence actions, the troops were advised to fire only when they could see the whites of the enemy's eyes—a range of about 30 metres!

57 Pair of pistols made by European gunsmiths for the eastern market in the early nineteenth century. The butts are of the ball-type, the locks are inlaid with mother-of-pearl and the barrels engraved; the locks are of the waterproof type.

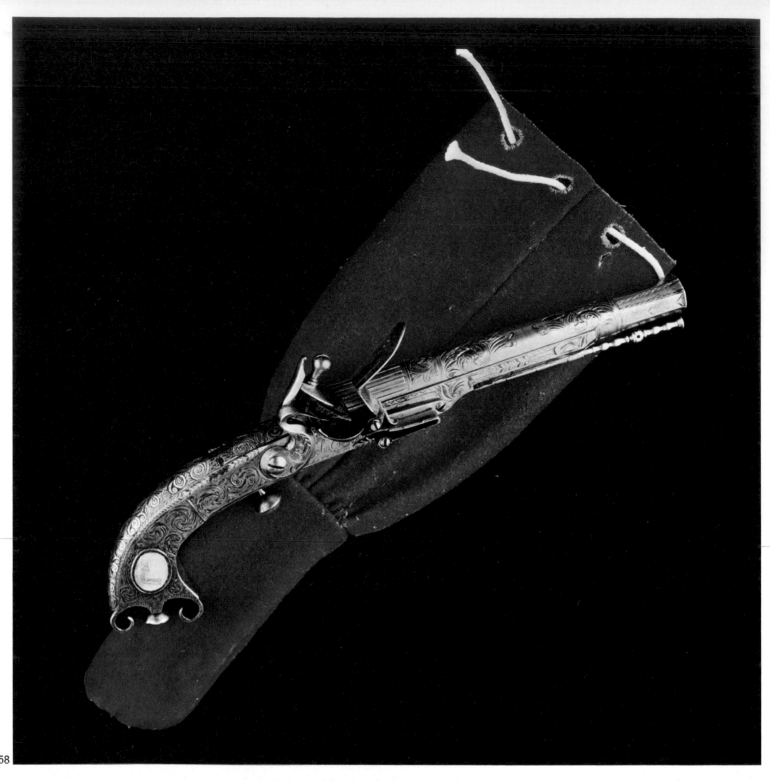

58

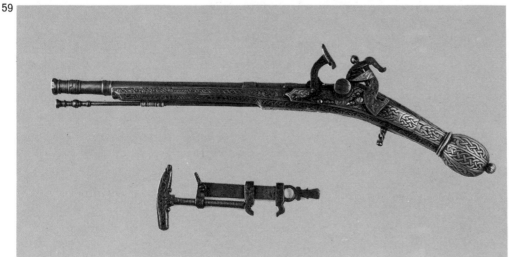

59

58 Scottish flint-lock pistol with a thick cloth travelling bag. It is signed Campbell and may date from about 1780. It is a typical Scottish arm with the characteristics which marked these pistols up to about 1830: a knob trigger without trigger guard; butt ending in a ram's horn; a needle for cleaning out the touch-hole, which slips in between the two horns; metal lock silvered all over, and a panel for the arms of the owner. In Scotland there were many good gunmakers, especially at Doune.

59 Reproduction Scottish pistol of the beginning of the seventeenth century, with Dutch-type 'snaaphaans' lock marked 1610 on the knob of the pan. These pistols had no trigger-guard, and this example has a lemon butt. The barrel is ornate; the stock is of brass. Under the pistol is a combination tool for flint-locks, consisting of a little hammer for shaping flints, a screwdriver, and a clamp for compressing the mainspring so that the lock can be taken to pieces.

60 Pair of English flint-lock pistols of the type called 'Queen Anne', about 1760, and a metal powder-flask, about 1850. 'Queen Anne' pistols came into use in England at the beginning of the eighteenth century and are characterized by the barrel, in the form of a miniature cannon; silver plate decoration on the ball of the butt; barrel made to unscrew for loading, and the absence of any wooden forestock. The turn-off barrel places them in the semi-breech-loading class. When the barrel, which extended as far as the chamber, was removed, the chamber was filled with powder on which the bullet was placed and the barrel screwed on again: the latter was of slightly smaller bore than the chamber, which prevented the bullet falling down the bore. Pistols with turn-off barrels were made in many countries.

61 Semi-breech-loading by means of turn-off barrels was much used in little single and double pocket pistols, like those shown here. (Their Italian name, *mazzagatti,* literally means 'cat-killers'.) At the top is a double-barrelled over-and-under pocket pistol, with two cocks, Belgian made, from the end of the eighteenth century, as are the other two. The second has four barrels, each with its own lock and with two hammers: when the upper pair of barrels had been fired, the block was rotated and the two unfired barrels were thus brought under the hammers which were cocked again. All three pistols have metal butts.

62 Pair of Belgian pocket pistols of the second half of the eighteenth century, signed H. Devillers à Liège. The fine quality butts have chiselled scrolls of rococo type against a gilt ground; the turn-off barrels are of cannon type, also with gilt decoration.

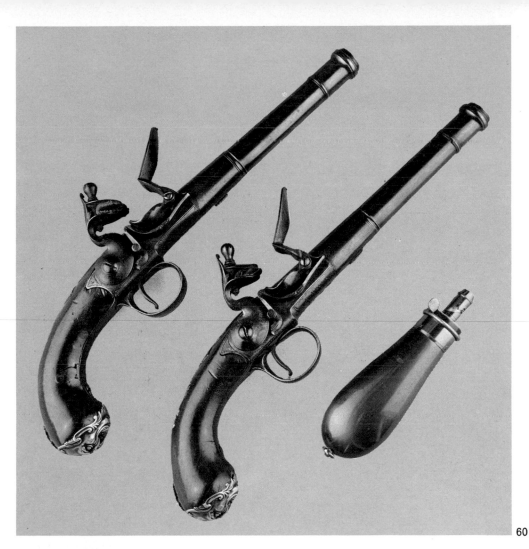

60

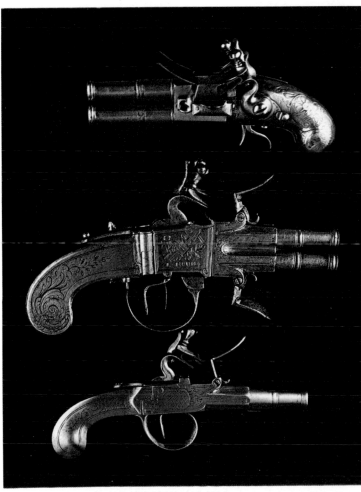

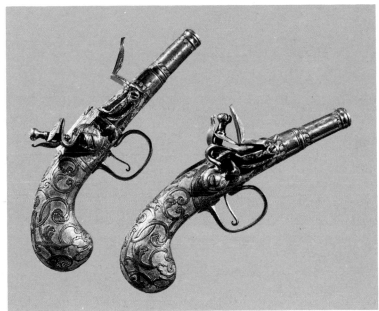

61   62

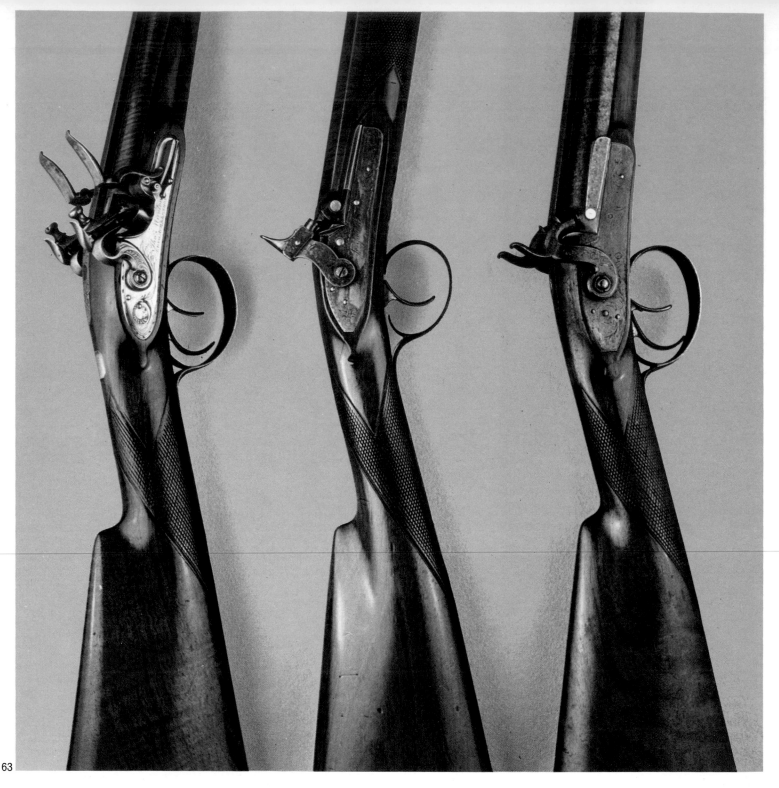

63

64

63 Three English sporting guns of the first decade of the nineteenth century. They bear the name Manton, gunmakers of London; the younger, Joseph, who was active from 1795 to 1835, is reckoned one of the best arms makers of all time. The double-barrelled gun on the left is dated about 1815, and has waterproof flint-locks with spoon-shaped pans. The second is a single-barrelled percussion gun of about 1830. The third is a double-barrelled percussion gun, also of about 1830–1835. The last two arms are by Joseph Manton. Note, in the double guns, the top-ribs, i.e. the reinforcing rib patented by Joseph Manton in 1806 and still in use today. The proportions and form of the butt are also practically the same as those of modern double guns. The modern sporting gun may be said to have been originated by Joseph Manton.

64 Flint-lock of about 1820, signed by the Milanese gunmaker Colombo. It is of the waterproof type then in vogue in England and France.

65

66

65 Pair of percussion breech-loading pistols by Johannes Samuel Pauly. Pauly, a Swiss, patented his invention in France in 1812. It consists of a metal cartridge case which was filled with powder on which was placed the bullet. The whole was then inserted in the breech of the gun. On the base of the case, communicating with the powder inside through a hole, was a fulminate cap, which, when the breech had been closed, was struck by an internal hammer cocked by a dummy one on the outside. The cases can be seen here, but these have been modified for thimble caps.

66 Robert breech-loading pistol of about 1830, shown with the breech open. A cartridge was inserted into the breech, this being composed of a small cylinder of inflammable paper containing bullet and powder, with a small tube filled with fulminate at the rear end. When the breech was closed and the trigger pressed, an internal hammer or firing-pin struck the tube.

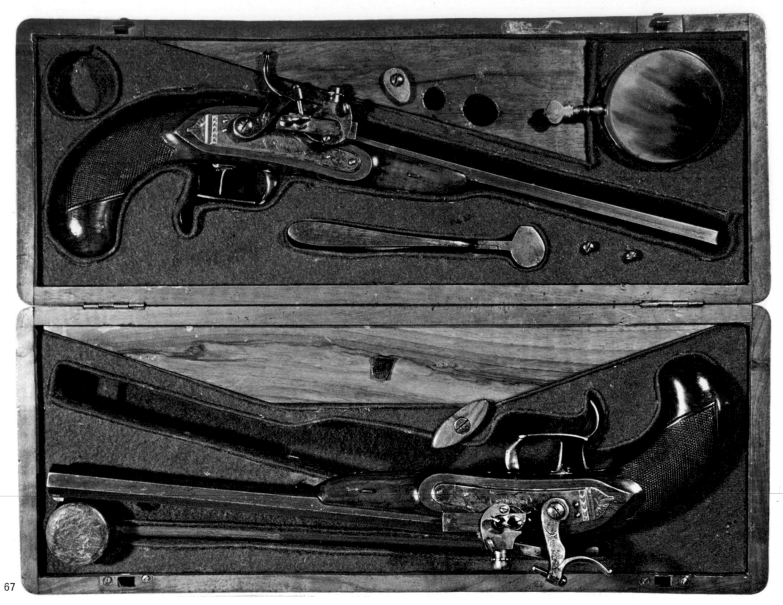

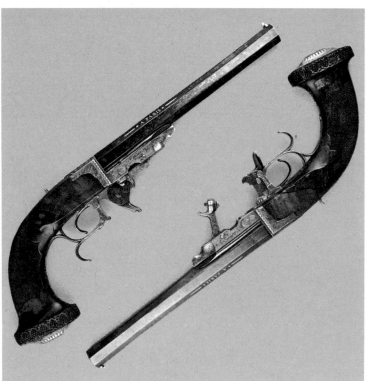

67 Case of duelling pistols with Contriner system percussion locks. This system practically repeated that patented by the Spaniard Gutierrez in the first half of the nineteenth century. The cock is connected by a cam with the fulminate container which slides on a horizontal guide, the end of which nearest the hammer has a recess opposite the touch hole. When the cock was raised, the container slid along the guide and its open end came in contact with the recess, into which a charge of fulminate powder fell. When the trigger was pressed, the hammer fell and, through the cam, moved the container, uncovering the recess into which the firing-pin at the end of the hammer fell. In the upper pistol the hammer is shown down: in the one below, the hammer is up and the fulminate container is over the recess. The pistols are muzzle-loading and have rifled barrels.

68 Pair of percussion pistols on Gossiet's system, using a pellet of fulminate. The hammer is below the barrel; the outside touch hole terminates in a recess, in which a pellet of fulminate was placed, after lifting the movable cover of the recess. When the cover, in which a firing pin was fitted, was closed, and the trigger pressed, the hammer descended on the firing-pin and exploded the pellet, firing the charge. They have muzzle-loading, rifled barrels. This pair, like the previous one, is of about 1820: both examples represent the efforts of the gunmakers of the period to personalize the percussion system invented by the reverend Alexander Forsyth, a Scottish minister.

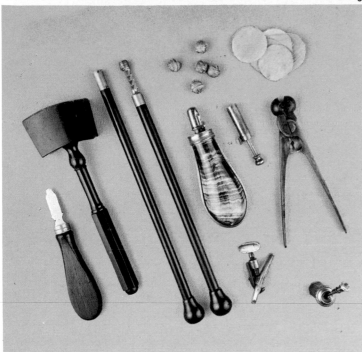
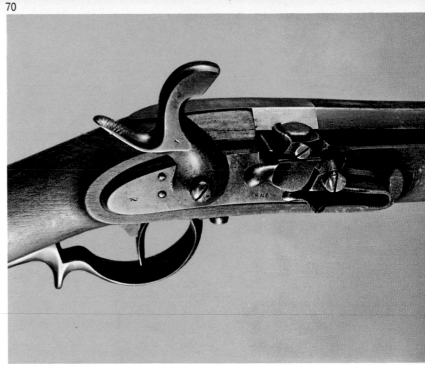

69 Set of accessories for loading rifled muzzle-loading pistols, especially duelling pistols, of the early nineteenth century. Duelling with pistols had already enjoyed a period of great popularity in the reign of George III. It reached a zenith at the end of the eighteenth century and became almost a fashion in the nineteenth, especially during the first twenty years of the century. This explains the large production of duelling pistols in those years and also the perfection and elegance of these weapons, which were supplied complete with accessories for loading and maintenance. From left to right and from top to bottom in the photograph can be seen screwdrivers; wooden mallet for driving the bullet down the rifled barrel with the aid of the ramrod; ramrod; barrel cleaning rod; leaden bullets wrapped in leather to take the rifling; horn and brass powder flask; clamp for removing mainsprings; small graduated measure for powder (beside the flask); cotton wads for wrapping round the bare bullet to ensure that it would take the rifling; pincer-type bullet-mould; oil can. Duelling pistols were rifled on the Continent, but smooth-bore in England.

70 Austrian military musket with percussion system using a small tube of fulminate, adapted by the Milanese Giuseppe Console and adopted by Austria for various types of arms from 1837 to 1850. This was the first application of an invention patented by Joseph Manton in 1818. Opposite the touch hole, in place of the pan, was a recess in which a small copper tube filled with fulminate was inserted. A cover was then closed over the tube, and on this the hammer fell when the trigger was pressed.

71 Inside view of two typical military musket actions of the middle nineteenth century. The upper has a back-action lock. The lower has a side action and is an adaptation of a flint-lock arm to the percussion system.

72 Two military percussion rifles of about the middle nineteenth century. Above; a Piedmontese double-barrelled musket used by the Sardinian carabinieri. Below, a Belgian carbine with the Delvigne bullet insertion system: the part of the breech in which the chamber was formed was of smaller bore than the barrel. The bullet was battered against the lands with the ramrod until it entered the grooving.

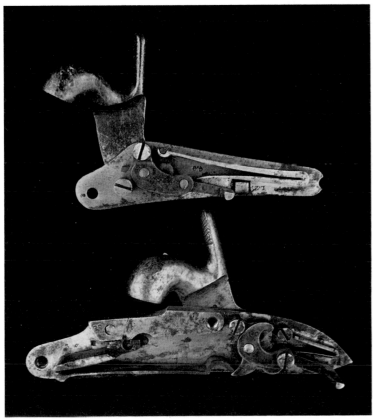

73 Breech-loading Italian flint-lock gun dated 1664 on the lock. This is one of the oldest breech-loading systems. The breech opens like a tobacco-box, and a cartridge case containing powder and bullet is inserted into the barrel. This case has a hole at one side opposite the touch hole. The cartridge case is the part seen above the arm. The system was a practicable one (a match-lock arquebus of Henry VIII of England was fitted with it), and if a good stock of cases were available, it was possible to fire many shots in rapid succession. However, the gas seal was imperfect; apart from the danger of burns, the arm was very irregular at long range because of the loss of pressure in the barrel.

74 Piedmontese breech-loading wall gun of the first half of the nineteenth century. This weapon, too, has a tobacco-box breech action. It is a percussion arm, and the nipple can be seen clearly in the breech. The gun was originally a flint-lock. The pan was later removed and the action modified with the addition of a new hammer. 'Wall arms' is the term applied to blunder-busses, arquebuses, and small swivel-guns, larger and heavier than usual, which were fired from a swivel on the top of a breastwork. They were placed at strategic points on fortifications, or distributed along a wall for defence at close quarters. The type designed to project a single bullet were sometimes as much as 30 millimetres bore.

75 Breech-loading flint-lock dated 1831, made at the Naples Royal Arms Factory. It is practically identical with the weapon which the American John H. Hall had patented in his own country in 1811, and was adopted for some special corps of the US army. However, it cannot be said that the Naples factory copied this: in fact, Hall's gun is identical with that patented by the owner of a French arms factory, the widow Guerin, in the last years of the eighteenth century, and offered by her, in vain, to Napoleon. The Guerin system was also based on a moving breech block, which, however, had the special feature of being integral with the lock. Like that of Crespi, this turned on a pin at the back (it can be seen here standing up between the two screws under the head of the hammer). This system, however, like the others already described, did not give a perfect gas seal, with all the consequences of this defect, and was therefore unsuccessful.

76 Piedmontese flint-lock of 1752, converted to breech-loading. The breech block is hinged to the rest of the barrel. To load, the breech block was rotated, powder and bullet inserted and the breech block restored to position and locked with the handle seen in this plate. The priming was placed in the pan and the arm was then ready to fire. This system recalls that of the Milanese, Francesco Crespi, adopted by Austria in 1770 for some of their special corps. In Crespi's breech-loader, the breech block moved back and turned upward on a pin in its base.

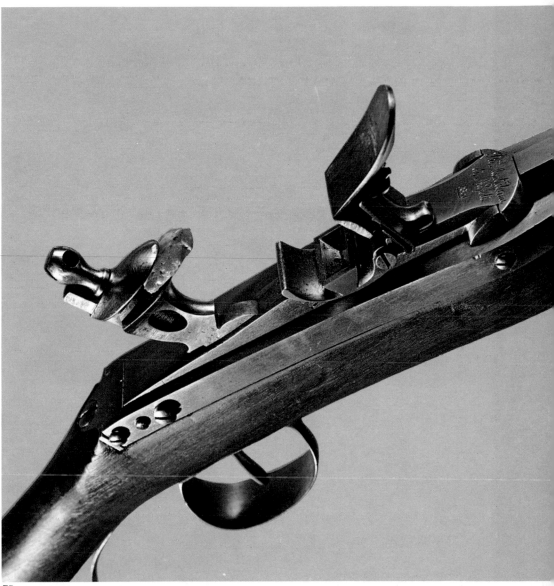

75

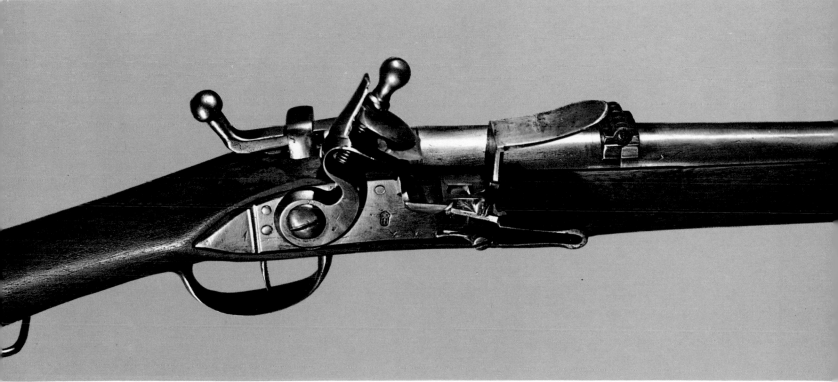

76

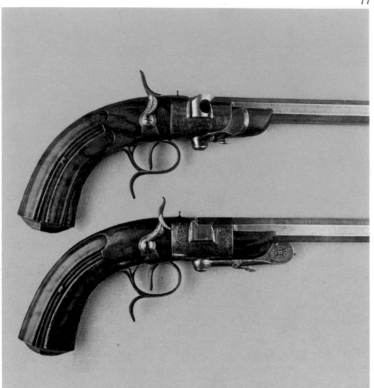

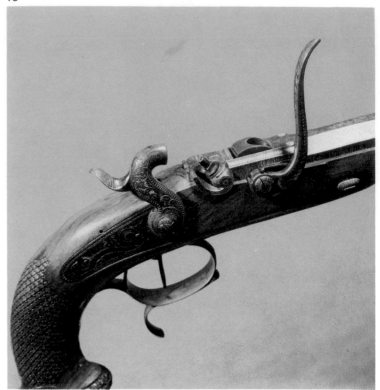

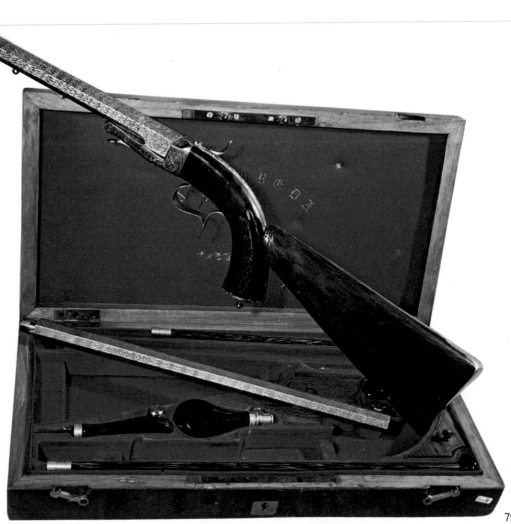

77 A pair of breech-loading percussion pistols of about 1840. These are by the Milanese gunsmith Colombo, who operated during the first half of the nineteenth century, and was famous for the excellent workmanship of his weapons. Moving the lever under the barrel rotated the breech end of the latter together with the primer and chamber, in which powder and bullet were placed. The pistols have rifled barrels, French type of butt, and internal hammer.

78 Pistol, one of a pair, by the French maker Lelyon. In this, too, loading was carried out as in Colombo's pistols, with the difference that the breech block rotated vertically and not in the horizontal plane, as with the foregoing types. About 1840.

79 A very beautiful case with a pistol-carbine set, signed Lebeda; percussion system. The pistol barrel unscrews and can be replaced with a longer one. A stock can be fitted to the grip of the pistol, as seen here. The damascened barrels are of magnificent workmanship. It dates from about 1840.

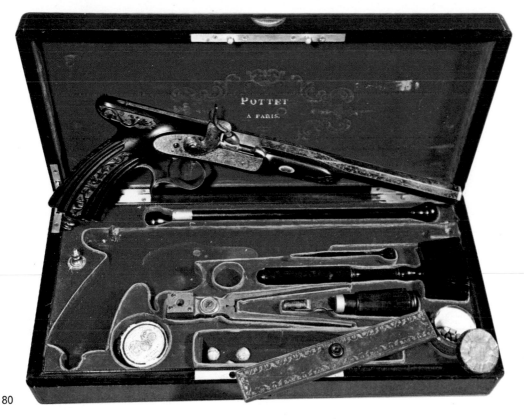

80

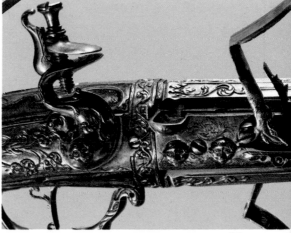

82

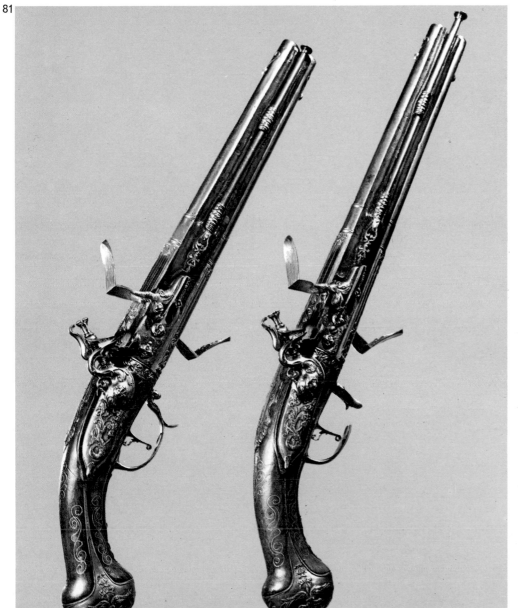

81

80 Case and pistol, complete with accessories, by the Parisian maker Pottet, about 1830. The pistol has an ebony saw-handle butt. As it is a percussion super-imposed arm, there are two nipples; the front one is horizontal, and is struck by a small bar fixed to an extension of the neck of the hammer; the other, which is oblique, is struck by the head of the hammer. Though a percussion weapon, the arm has one of the oldest repeating systems.

81–82 Pair of Italian superimposed load pistols of Wender type from the late seventeenth century, with two revolving barrels, each with its own lock and three touch holes to fire three successive charges in each barrel. Though one of the problems for which the old gunsmiths was an efficient breech-loading system, another, no less important, problem offered a field for a wide variety of experiments—that of a repeating action. In this pair of pistols, this difficulty has been solved: more power has been given to the arm by fitting each weapon with two barrels (multi-barrel system) and arranging that each barrel could fire three successive charges (superimposed charge system). In plate 82 can be seen, with the lock cocked, the pan which extends beyond the pin of the action: three touch holes open into this pan, and are closed by small movable shutters which are moved by operating two plates at the side of the screw and lifting a third cover on the right of the hammer (the outline can be seen). The charges were loaded one upon another opposite each touch hole. When the first had been fired, the second touch hole opened and the pan was primed again, and so, in the same way, for the third. The pair, made by an Italian gunsmith, have walnut stocks decorated with silver wire inlay. The furniture and lock plates are in iron with typical Italian chiselled decoration.

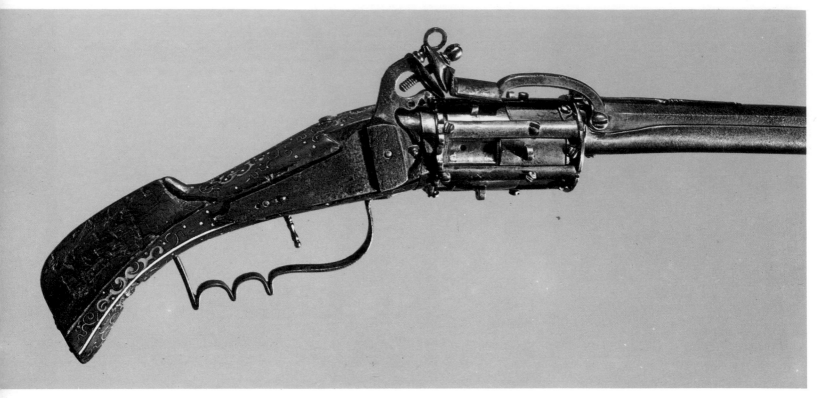

83 Large revolving flint-lock pistol of the end of the sixteenth century. Each chamber in the cylinder has a pan, touch hole and pan cover moved by hand. There is a single lock with cock and trigger on the butt of the arm, and the steel is hinged to the barrel. The frizzen lacks the steel. The butt is decorated with metal and bone inlay work. The arm is rather long, about 80 centimetres. The chambers are, of course, loaded from the front; the barrel is smooth bore. This arm is notable for good workmanship and the intelligent use of the cylinder system—the cylinder was turned by hand after each shot.

84 Three-shot German flint-lock pistol of 1730–1740. Here, too, the cylinder system is used. Three chambers are formed in a revolving block between barrel and butt. Each chamber has its own touch hole with pan and frizzen (steel and pan cover). There is only one barrel. The cylinder was turned by hand. At the beginning of the nineteenth century, the American Elisha Collier, who worked in London, constructed a flint-lock revolver in which the pans of the chambers were automatically primed with fine powder. A small magazine of priming powder was formed in the hammer, which opened to allow a little powder to fall into the pan each time it came down. Samuel Colt seems to have taken the idea for his first revolver from Collier's pistol.

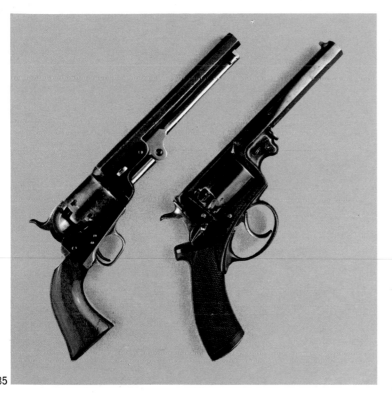

85 Two typical nineteenth century percussion revolvers. On the left, the Colt Navy revolver, 1851 model, .36 calibre. On the right, the Adams-Beaumont 1855 model, .44 calibre. The former is one of the most famous Colt arms, which was also made in the London branch of the American Hartford works. The latter is English, and shows in its very elegant lines the good taste of the British gunmakers. The cylinder is loaded from the front with a cartridge (composed of inflammable paper containing the powder, followed by the bullet). The nipples on which the copper percussion caps were placed can be seen. The Model 1851 Colt was one of the favourite arms of the cavalry during the American Civil War. The pistol is single-action: the hammer had to be cocked for each shot by drawing it back with the thumb. This action rotated the cylinder (Colt's innovation in 1836). The Adams-Beaumont, on the contrary, is a double-action pistol, i.e. it was cocked not only in the same way as the Colt, but also by pressing the trigger, which cocked the lock, rotated the cylinder, and, when the trigger reached the end of its travel, released the hammer.

86–87 English percussion gun of 1850–1860 by Joseph Enouy of London, with two revolving cylinders: it fired 12 shots, six from each cylinder. Plate 87 shows how the cylinders rotate to bring the charges under the hammer in succession.

85

86

87

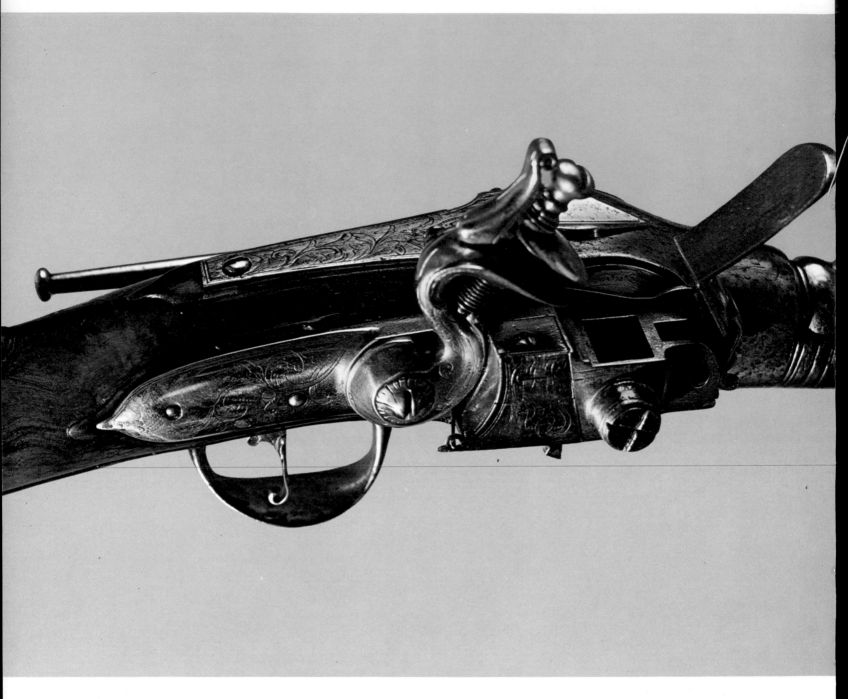

88 Flint-lock repeating gun on the Lorenzoni system, signed Berselli in Bologna, about 1680. This is a beautiful example of this type of arm, which may be considered the only true flint-lock repeater. Two cylindrical magazines were formed in the stock, one for powder, the other for bullets. There were 24 charges. The following can be clearly seen here: the lever on the left hand side of the arm, which turns a brass drum which picks up powder and bullet (this can be seen projecting behind the barrel extension); the small priming magazine between the pan and the cock; the cam which connects the frizzen (steel and pan cover) to the drum, and also connects the neck of the cock to the latter. The two cams raise the cock and lower the frizzen over the pan when the revolving breech is rotated to receive the bullet and powder. The barrel is smooth-bore.

89 Three repeating pistols with lever actions, origin of the famous American Winchester 66. The one on the left is by the Italian gunsmith Venditti di Langusi, and dates from about 1870: the second is the American Volcanic by the Volcanic Repeating Arms Company, formed in 1855, whose principal shareholder was Oliver Winchester; six-inch barrel, calibre .40. The third is also a Volcanic, but of pocket type with a four-inch barrel. From these arms, through the Henry carbine of 1860, the Winchester 66 was derived: this retained the loading mechanism and the tubular magazine under the barrel. In the Volcanic, the cartridge was pushed into an opening near the muzzle: in the Winchester

there was a small door in the frame through which the cartridges were pushed into the magazine. The Volcanic cartridge was quite peculiar. It used the 'rocket-ball', invented by the American Hunt, and consisted of an ogival ball, in the base of which was a recess in which a charge of black powder was placed. The recess was then closed with a perforated disc of felt or leather: the flash from an ordinary percussion cap passed through this. The Volcanic 'rocket-ball', however, was rather different: instead of the powder, there was a charge of fulminate of mercury, and the primer was incorporated, so that it could be struck with a firing pin in the breech block. The cartridges were thus fed into the chamber by moving the lever up and down: this lever formed the trigger guard and terminated in a loop. This same action is to be found in the Winchester. It should be noted that Volcanic Repeating Arms Company was originally Smith and Wesson, two other great names in the history of American arms, founded in 1854 and then sold to a group of businessmen including Oliver Winchester. Subsequently the firm became the property of Winchester alone and took his name, which it still retains.

90 An English four-barrelled flint-lock pistol of the end of the eighteenth century. When the first two barrels had been fired it was only necessary to turn the tap-action lever, seen here, to bring the primed pans of the two lower barrels into position, so that these could be fired in their turn.

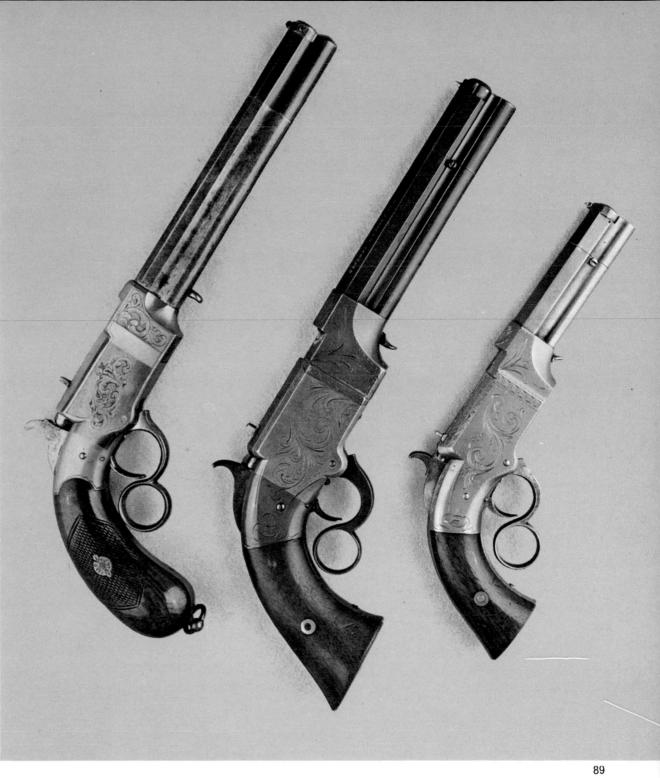

88

89

90

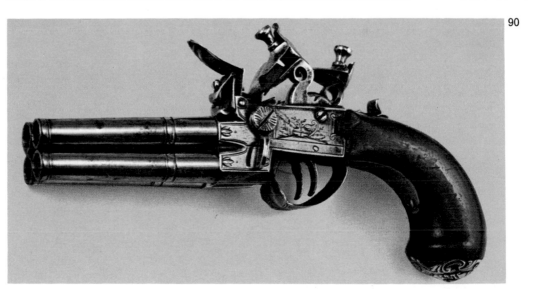

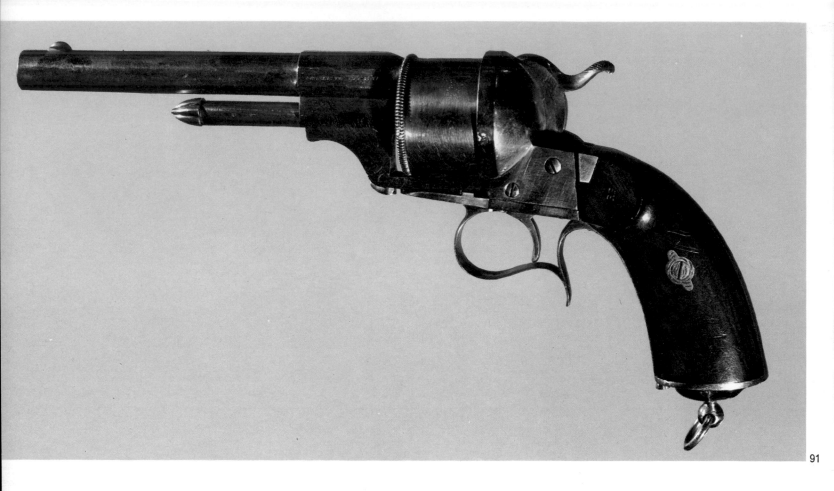

91

91 Military revolving pistol on the Lefaucheux pin-fire system, adopted by Piedmont about 1860. Its lines show the derivation from the French Lefaucheux revolving pistol. Calibre 11 millimetres; single action (the hammer must be cocked with the thumb for each shot). This was the first revolving pistol used in the Italian Army in which it was replaced by a new model only in 1874, viz. the Chamelot-Delvigne 11 millimetres central-fire revolver.

92 An English pin-fire revolver by Field of Oxford, about the middle of the nineteenth century. This fires merely by pressing the trigger, which rotates the cylinder, cocks the hammer and then releases it without any interruption. Sighting with such arms was, however, somewhat problematical. This revolver, which was probably an adaptation of the 'pepper-box' revolver (a revolving pistol with a number of barrels grouped in cylindrical form, instead of a cylinder) shows what efforts were made to adapt new discoveries to old weapons. To extract the spent cartridge cases and reload, the cylinder was released and slid out on its long central pin.

93 Pin-fire revolving pistol, about 1860–1870. Double-action, with open frame and walnut grips, it bears the Liège proof marks. The extractor pin is missing. Calibre 9 millimetres.

94–95 Dreyse military rifle, 1841 model. This is the first firearm with a sliding breech block and needle-fire. Johann Nikolaus von Dreyse invented the breech-loading system used in this arm in 1828. After several modifications, the rifle was examined by the Prussian Army in 1841 with great interest, but was only adopted in 1848. The Prussian Army was the first in the world to have a breech-loading rifle as its standard weapon. In plate 94 the arm is seen with the breech closed, and in 95 with the breech open. The long 'needle' which acted as firing-pin is missing. The defects of this weapon were the escape of gas at the breech and the corrosion of the needle, which, being exposed completely to the explosion of the charge, was liable to rapid wear. However, the weapon remained in service for more than 20 years.

92   93

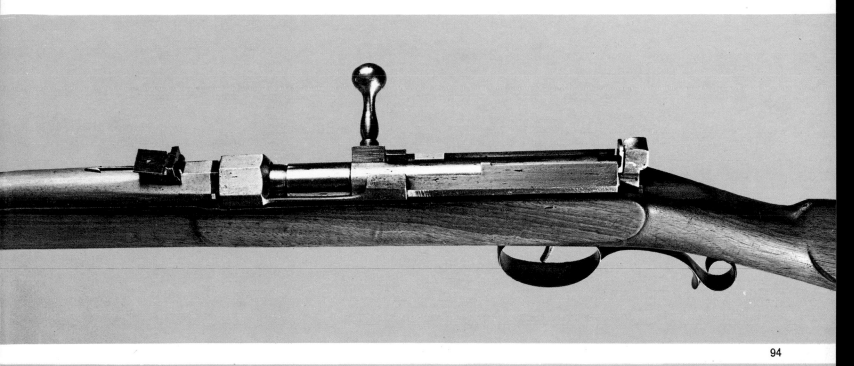

94

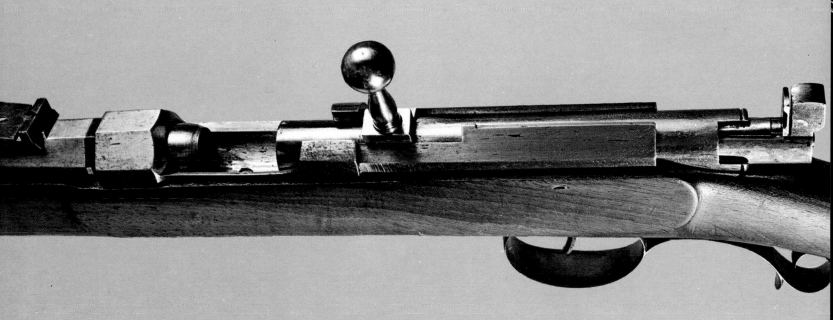

95

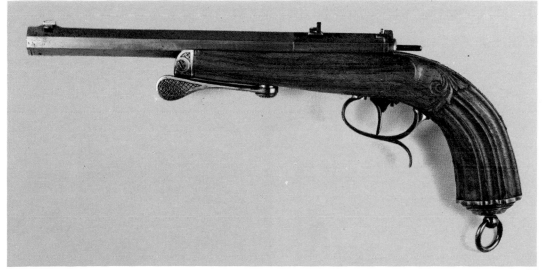

96 Dreyse system breech-loading pistol, about 1850. This is a clever application of the 'needle-fire' system: to load, the lever under the breech was turned and the barrel dropped down, opening the breech for loading. The small bar projecting behind showed that the arm was ready to fire.

96

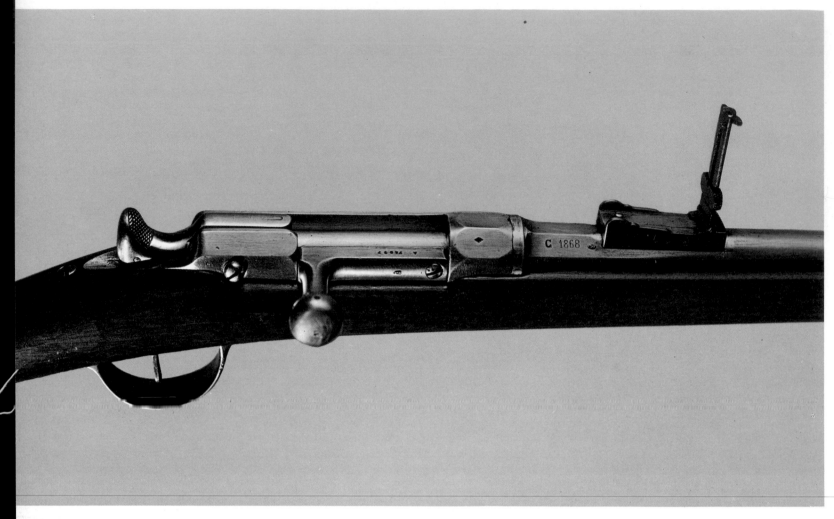

97–98 French Chassepot needle-fire military
rifle, 1866 model. The Frenchman, Antoine
Alphonse Chassepot, invented his rifle in 1863: it
was inspired by the Dreyse 'needle-gun'. It was
adopted by France in 1866 and remained in service
until 1874, when the Gras rifle, using a metal
cartridge case and central-fire, superseded it. The
Chassepot is an improvement on the Dreyse, as
the needle was a true firing pin which struck a
percussion cap at the base of the cartridge:
further, the sliding breech block had a rubber seal
at the end which, compressed against the standing
breech, expanded and reduced the escape of gas.
However, after a certain number of shots, the heat
of the breech melted the rubber, with the
consequences which might be expected. In plate
98, which shows the breech open, the rubber seal
can be seen.

99

100

99–100 Italian needle-gun, Carcano model. The years from 1865 to 1870 saw the nations of Europe faced with the need to modernize their small-arms. The American Civil War (1861–1865), which was fought mainly by troops armed with muzzle-loading percussion weapons, was marked by the appearance on the battlefield of a wide range of breech-loading arms, with metal cartridges, and the end of the nipple and cap system. In Italy, the armaments were renovated, but as cheaply as possible, by modifying the muzzle-loading weapons to breech-loading by the system devised by an engineer of the Turin Arsenal, Salvatore Carcano. The barrels were relined, cut off at the breech and adapted to Carcano's rotary-sliding breech action, which was simple and cheap to produce. As in the Chassepot, the firing pin was short and struck a cap at the base of the paper cartridge. The chief features of the Carcano breech action were still retained in the 1891 repeating arm. Carcano's needle action, which can be seen here with breech closed and open, was adopted in 1868. The single shot Vetterli took its place two years later, using metal cartridges, 1870 model.

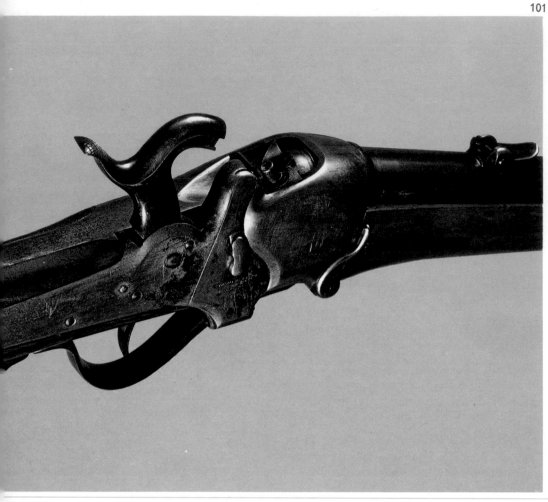

101 American Sharp's 1851 model, breech-loading percussion carbine. The nineteenth century offered many solutions to the problem of loading an arm at the breech. One was that of Christian Sharp who, in 1848, patented his rifle, in which the breech block moved vertically, being opened for loading by a lever which also formed a trigger guard. In this 1851 model, the rifle is seen fitted with Maynards taper priming mechanism, consisting of a magazine from which, when the hammer was lowered, a ribbon of pellets of fulminate issued in the direction of the nipple. The cartridge of Sharp's carbine had the usual consumable paper case containing powder and bullet. When the breech closed, the sharp angle of the breech block cut open the base of the cartridge as it rose, thus exposing the powder to the flash of the cap.

102 Peabody-Martini rifle, with hinged breech block and central-fire metal cartridge. When the trigger-guard is lowered, as in Sharp's carbine, the breech block drops down to expose the standing breech. A groove in the block makes it easier to insert the cartridge. The Martini-Henry, a similar type of rifle, was the British Victorian colonial weapon of the last decades of the nineteenth century.

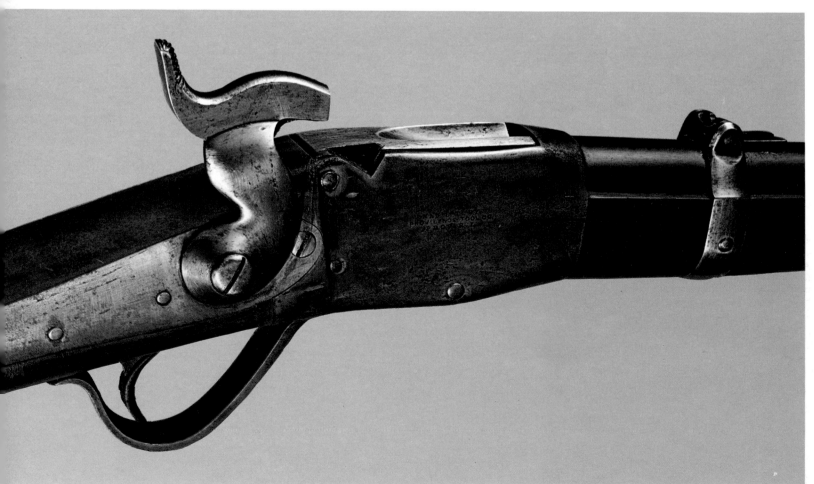

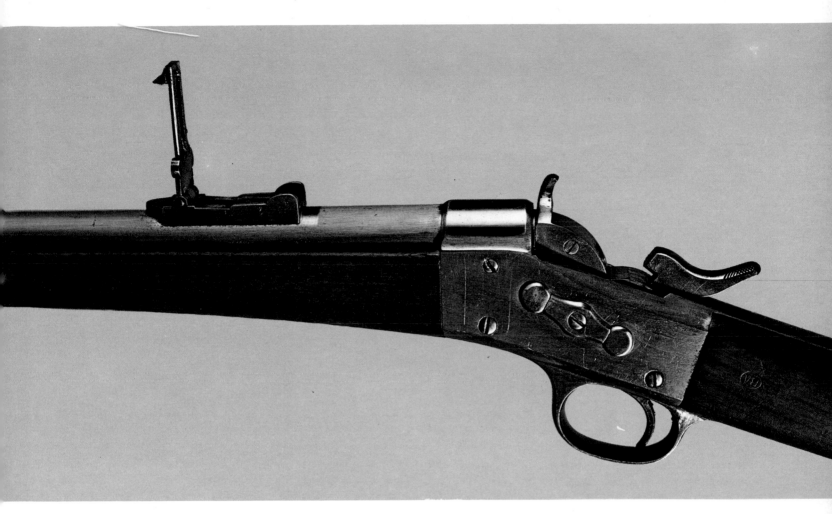

103

104

103–104 Remington 1867 model rolling-block, single shot, metal cartridge centre fire rifle. The American, Eliphalet Remington, already known for his invention of an efficient percussion revolver between 1855 and 1860, invented in 1864 a rifle based on a breech action termed the rolling-block. This was simple and functional. The breech block and hammer turned on two pivots, parallel but lying in different planes. When the hammer was raised and the breech block turned backward, the chamber was opened for loading. When the cartridge had been inserted and the breech block turned forward again, the rifle was ready to fire. When the hammer fell, its pressure, and the fact that it was pivoted in a different plane from that of the breech block, locked the latter to the standing breech. In plate 103, the arm is seen with the hammer down; in 104 the breech block is also lowered, opening the breech for loading. The system met with approval all over the world, and the rifle was adopted by many European nations.

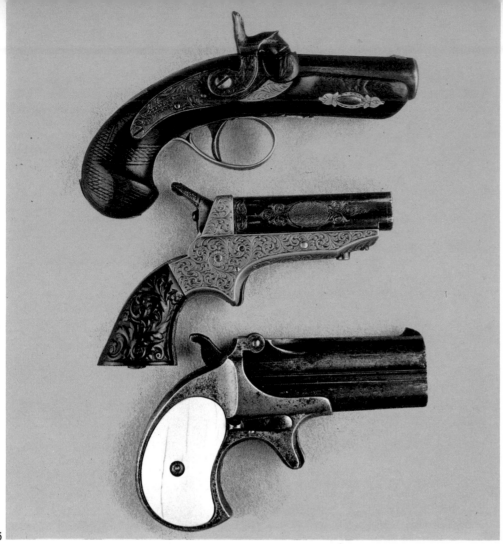

105

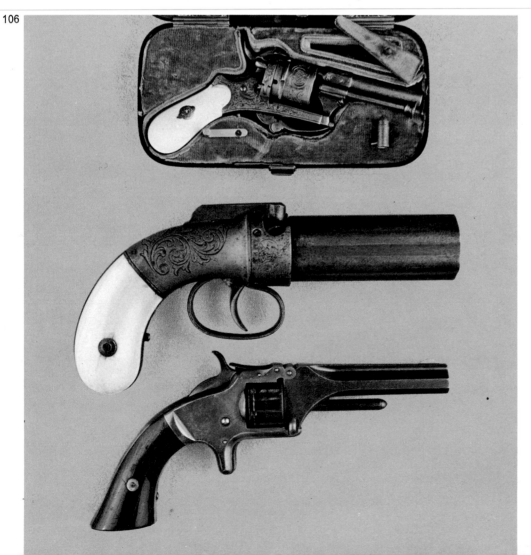

106

105 From the top: Derringer muzzle-loading rifled percussion pocket pistol; Sharp's breech-loading four-barrel percussion revolving pistol for rim-fire metal cartridges, .22 calibre (5.6 millimetres); and a Remington Derringer with under-and-over barrels for rim-fire metal cartridges, .41 calibre. These three arms practically summarize the history of the American Pocket pistol from 1850 (Derringer muzzle-loader) to 1859–1866 (Sharp's four-barrelled pistol and Remington's 'Double Derringer'). The muzzle-loading pistol was made by Henry Derringer, a Philadelphia gunsmith, and was very popular about 1850, especially among gamblers. It also gained sad battle honours when John Wilkes Booth assassinated President Abraham Lincoln with one, on the 14th April 1865. The success of the Derringer was such that it found a host of imitators who marketed similar arms under the name of 'Derringer' (one more error). The name thus meant a pocket pistol for defence and offence at short range. The name was taken up again by Remington for their 'Double Derringer' in 1866. This arm was made from 1865 to 1935, and copies of it are still produced, evidence of its success. The Sharp's four-barrel revolving percussion pistol, on the other hand, appeared as a competitor to the 'pepperbox' pocket pistol.

106 From the top: European ladies' pin-fire revolver of about 1880; American Allen and Thurber 'pepperbox' revolver, about 1850; .22 rim-fire Smith and Wesson No. 1 revolver, second type, 1860. The 'pepperbox' in the centre is one of the most elegant of revolving-barrel arms; this one is a six-barrelled weapon, muzzle-loading and with percussion nipples. When the trigger is pressed, the group of barrels revolves and the hammer rises to its fullest extent and then falls on the nipple. The Allen and Thurber 'pepperbox' revolvers, however, gave way to the Colt and later to the rim-fire metal cartridge revolvers of Smith and Wesson, which gained wide popularity as soon as they appeared. The pin-fire revolver is shown in its tortoiseshell case covered with velvet—a luxury weapon of elegant workmanship, with ivory grips.